Multiple Streams
of Success
Real life stories of faith,
hope, success, and
overcoming adversity

Mark Johnson, Editor

Olmstead Publishing

4th of July 2008

Multiple Streams of Success: Real life stories of faith, hope, success, and overcoming adversity
Mark A Johnson, Editor
Authors: Margaret Myrick Ingram, Gary Hagen, Pam Rodgers, Don Sepulveda, Dr. Isaac Deas, Michael Fuchs, Ken Scrubbs, Al Coury, Dr. Phyllis M Olmstead, Robin Andre Rodrigue, Mark A Johnson

Copyright 4th of July 2008

Olmstead Publishing

olmsteadllc@usa.com

1631 Rock Springs Rd

Apopka, FL 32712-2229

Printed in the United States of America

Cover Illustrator Chris Hammett
clhammett@empowercreativeservices.com

ISBN-13   978-1-934194-11-9
ISBN-10   1-934194-11-5

This book is dedicated
in loving memory of my hero,
James Lee Johnson,
March 3, 1935 – June 23, 2008

And to the

Alive Hospice Staff
whose compassion helped
celebrate his homecoming.

Table of Contents

Acknowledgments 5
Forward 7
A Tiny Miracle...Nakita Taylor 11
    Margaret Myrick Ingram
A Voice in the Dark 27
    Gary Hagen
A Conversation with God! 37
    Pam Rodgers
A Mother's Wounds A Child's Anguish God's Grace . 56
    Don Sepulveda
I Am Still Rising 71
    Isaac Deas
God Likes Me! 95
    Michael Fuchs
Some Say Money Doesn't Fall From the Sky—I Beg to
Differ! 112
    Ken Scrubbs
Follow Your Heart But Use Your Head 128
    Al Coury
Can I Motivate You? 158
    Phyllis M Olmstead
Rasselas Revisited 169
    Robin Andre Rodrigue
Impacting the Space I Occupy 192
    Mark Anthony Johnson

Acknowledgments

FIRST AND FOREMOST, I ACKNOWLEDGE GOD FOR NOT QUIETING THE INNER VOICE THAT PROMPTED ME FORWARD IN THIS ENDEAVOR, MY WIFE AND FAMILY FOR THEIR ENCOURAGEMENT, AND MY COAUTHORS, WHOSE WILLINGNESS TO BE VULNERABLE MADE THIS DREAM POSSIBLE.
To my friends and associates who have supported me, both directly and indirectly, in helping make this dream come true. I want to thank my brothers and sisters of the Foliage Toastmasters Club in Apopka, FL. This club served as an incubator of learning and evaluation. Especially Rudy St Cyr, whose edifying encouragement and brutal honesty is what true relationships require. I also want to thank Susie Gallucci, Amy Sellers, and Shelley Costello whose influences placed me in the right places at the right times in my life.

I would like to thank the many people who have contributed insights that have influenced my work as a life coach, speaker, author, and facilitator of change within the prison and local community. Specifically, Kevin Bracy, of LifeChangers International, who inspired me to impact those within the space I occupy through the use of positive words.

Les Brown, the powerful motivational speaker, who challenged me to 'Push Ups,' thus exposing my humility. I developed an appreciation for his essence; whose exhortation, "There is **Greatness Inside of Me**" continues to resonate within my spiritual and mental core. Marcia Wieder, Dream University®, my life coach mentor, whose powerful love and passion for purpose and achieving one's dreams continues to fuel me. In addition, I thank Vernice Armour, the first female African American Marine Corp combat pilot, whose continued distant words of support and encouragement planted me squarely in the Boys and Girls Club of Leesburg, FL. Doru Ghedeon Bere, thank you for your unique style of branding that created my DNA of **Life To The Brim** exemplifying my core life purpose.

A very special thanks to my friends David Duris, Chuck Schell, and Dr. Isaac Deas for being warriors of encouragement and to Pastor Terry Mahan and the men of the Father's House who, as my band of brothers, are always standing in the gap and not afraid of being men of compassion and strength.

Kudos to Dr. Phyllis Olmstead whose soft words of wisdom and direction served as a rudder keeping this ship going in the right direction. In addition, to the quiet and most humble Chris Hammett whose gift of design took my words and created a magnificent visual icon for all to see. Warden Carlye I. Holder (retired) for his heart and compassion in believing incarcerated men and woman can change if given the opportunity. His words at the **500 Men of Valor** event still cling to my soul. "I want to be all used up when I die," is a true testimony to what our life purpose should be.

Warden Archie Longley for consistently encouraging and supporting my purpose of impacting the space I occupy. And, of course, my vanpool partners who continue to endure my excessive talk of achieving greater heights through speaking.

Special blessings to those I have expressed gratitude for and to those I may not have mentioned. Life is a journey and we never travel it alone. There will always be someone else traveling along the path with us; it could be for one minute, week, month, year, or until the end. Whichever it is, enjoy the walk and appreciate the experience for it does not last forever.

Mark Johnson, editor

Forward

Last year I participated in a speaker workshop entitled First Step for Speakers. The event took place in Los Angeles, CA. Following the workshop was a speech contest entitled Speak Up—Speak Off. Three notable individuals judged all the contestants that advanced forward into the finals. I was one of the finalists. Following my presentation, each judge provided me valuable feedback. One judge, Ernie G. with a powerful essence of sincerity told me, "I loved your presentation, but I want to know about you, I want to know your story."

I placed second in that contest, and learned a great deal from the other contestants and judges, but what struck me the most was his comment regarding my story and loosening up. Being a passionate man, I tended to be rather intense during my presentations, lacking humor and never sharing my own story. I processed his feedback and understood the powerful impact sharing one's story has on those to which we communicate, being one or 100. By sharing our story, we reveal our vulnerabilities.

As a Toastmaster, I gained further knowledge regarding the powerful impact of story telling. People generally identify with vulnerability. Most people at some time in their life have experienced a significant emotional event, good or bad, that has had an impact on others through their sharing of it.

It is through our stories that others can see the manifestation of hope, faith, success, and our overcoming of adversity. It is through our stories that others can identify with pain, joy, and introspectively come to grips with their own issues. *Multiple Streams of Success: Real Life Stories of Faith, Hope, Success, and Overcoming Adversity* is an anthology of stories told by individuals who felt compelled to share their life experiences with others. This work took its own course reflecting the heart of each author and, ironically, becoming a spiritually inspiring entity. Kevin Bracy lit the match that ignited the idea of this work and an unassuming young woman in Port St. Lucie, FL, fanned it into a burning desire. Her story was so compelling that the idea of creating this work became an obsession, a dream, an intention.

Believe in your dreams, it is in your dreams that your passion lurks waiting for you to release it. When you release it, you will then be living in your purpose.

Mark Johnson

Nakita Taylor

is a life-long resident of Vero Beach, FL. Nakita is the youngest of five children being raised by her grandmother and two aunts.

Nakita is a public speaker whose focus is drug prevention and has received numerous accolades for speaking and community activism. She attends the Mueller Center at Indian River Community College in Vero Beach, FL. Nakita was recognized as one of the national Jefferson Award recipients in Washington, DC, representing the State of Florida.

Margaret Myrick Ingram

was born in the Graceville, FL. She was the ninth of eleven children, was educated in the public school system of Indian River County (IRCPS), and attended Indian River Community College in Ft Pierce, FL. She completed her undergraduate work at Florida Atlantic University in Boca Raton. She received the "Most Distinguish Award" at both schools.

Margaret began her career as an educator at Osceola Elementary in Vero Beach, FL. She attended Nova University in Ft Lauderdale where she received a Masters Degree in Administration and Supervision. She worked towards a doctoral degree in Early Childhood

Education until, then Governor Bob Graham, appointed her to serve as a Trustee on the Hospital Board in Indian River County. She served in this capacity for 13 years.

She received the following awards: Indian River County Teacher of the Year, Florida State Teacher of the Year, Christa McAuliffe Ambassador for Education, and Disney's Teacher of the Year.

Margaret Ingram is the founder and President of the Science Institute of Discovery, Inc. It is a Florida non-profit corporation dedicated to the purpose of inspiring minority students to become more interested, involved, and recognized in the field of science.

She teaches for Indian River County Public Schools, now in her 31st year. Her husband, George Ingram, Sr., serves as a Nuclear Assurance Lead Auditor at the St. Lucie Nuclear Plant. They have three sons.

Contact information: spider4b@aol.com

A Tiny Miracle

A little more than two decades ago, a tiny crack cocaine addicted infant was born. She was named Nakita Taylor. Weighing only about three pounds, unresponsive, without oxygen to the brain for about three minutes, and in severe respiratory distress, this infant was determined to live!

Imagine being born prematurely, addicted to a substance, and not expected to live. Nakita Taylor's journey into this world began in a cold, hard, filthy bathtub in an old dilapidated house. It is unimaginable the trauma her tiny infant body experienced as it faced a cruel and hostile world.

I cannot tell you why Nakita's mother chose to use illicit substances during her pregnancy, nor can I tell you how long she had been involved in using drugs. As fate would have it, one dreadful unexpected night, Niki's mother began experiencing excruciating pain. This pain was so intense that she crawled into a cold, hard, dirty bathtub to give birth to a precious gift from heaven.

As you know, a sterile environment is commonplace in our society when delivering a newborn. The lethal drug crack cocaine had robbed Nakita's mother of her God-given maternal instinct to call for help while delivering a baby. She was alone in an old abandoned house, crouched in a fetal position, with the hard cold bathtub being her only arms of comfort.

Against All Odds

The enemy's plan was to steal the mother and the baby she was carrying that night. However, what the enemy did not know was that God had another plan for that baby. Her mother's struggling soul cried up from the very pits of Hell, screaming an earsplitting sound to a 'ram in the bushes.' It was that magnanimous person, still unknown today, who called 911. In addition, divine intervention gave Nakita a glimmer of hope for an unlikely survival. The ambulance sped to the site and took the mother to the hospital where Niki was classified as an "at risk baby" and assigned a doctor who specialized in severe cases such as hers. Today Nakita Taylor is alive and miraculously on her way to an exciting future, by the grace of God!

After a turbulent battle with death, Niki's tiny little body gave up and surrendered to the divine will of

God! Nakita Taylor was to live and not die! Detached from her main source of crack cocaine delivered to her by her own mother through the umbilical cord, Niki found herself thrust into a seemingly hostile environment. With her tiny little limbs, drawn up into a fetal like position, she was screaming and crying for her next cocaine fix. These agonizing cravings went on until detoxification.

Niki's mother remained in the hospital for a while and was able to see her very tiny sick baby a few times. Like a thief, the call of cocaine beckoned her back to the streets. She left her tiny baby behind suffering from drug addiction to be cared for by total strangers. About a month and a few pounds later little Niki was ready to go home. The decision to bring this sick little baby home was not easy.

The Department of Child Services was going to place this abandoned crack baby in a foster home because the father was unknown and the maternal grandmother was afraid that she could not care for Niki due to her own illness. Grandmother's trips to dialysis treatments sapped her strength, making her too weak to care for a special needs baby. At this time, one of Niki's aunts stepped forward and volunteered to act as a surrogate mother. Niki was still so little that she had to sleep in a small dresser drawer taken from one of the pieces of furniture in the home. This prevented the tiny baby from falling out of the bed or from being rolled onto by the caregiver.

Upon the recommendation of medical personnel, Nakita entered the Infant Stimulation Program at the Association for Retarded Citizens (ARC). Due to the overload at ARC, visiting nurses provided the services at that site. These services were necessary as Niki was labeled as being of "High Developmental Risk" and diagnosed with partial Cerebral Palsy. Niki's gross and fine motor skills were significantly delayed. She required speech and language therapy, as well. She remained in the program at ARC from infancy until she was five years old. As time went on the baby grew stronger and stronger.

Seemingly, the task of caregiving proved to be too difficult for her aunt. Consequently, Niki had to move in with her sick grandmother where the aunt and other family members helped care for her. The family rallied around the growth and progress of this precious child. They also took her to church and kept her in the prayer line, believing that God would deliver her and

14

release her from this drawn-up fetal position and from the cocaine withdrawal tremors. Niki received a breakthrough! Prayers were answered! Thanks be to God, that the family and the church interceded on behalf of this very sick baby. The reports from the Infant Stimulation Program mimicked the same jubilant sentiments of praise concerning her progress.

Primary Education

At the age of five, Nakita Taylor entered a regular kindergarten. She entered school far behind other children her own age. Niki had a written Individual Educational Plan (IEP) and she received speech and occupational therapy, as well.

When she entered kindergarten, Niki knew between 15-20 words. In order for students to be successful in school at this level, their vocabularies should be vast, about 2000 words. As you can see, she was severely developmental delayed and disabled.

She walked with a limp, spoke with a slur, and sometimes drooled because she had not mastered control of all her muscles. Her disfigured right hand made it very difficult to grip a pencil correctly and made cutting next too impossible. Many normal children suffer all kinds of anxieties entering school for the first time, so for Niki this was another obstacle for her to overcome.

I am certain that the children stared at this lovely, beautifully dressed little girl with all the disabilities and had many questions about her unfamiliar behavior. They constantly teased her by pointing their fingers, laughing, and taunting her repeatedly, almost to the point that it became unbearable. Nevertheless, she continued at that school enduring this traumatic abuse until third grade.

Please keep in mind that Niki always considered others feeling above her own. Niki would not tell her grandmother because her grandmother was very ill and was also taking care of Niki's four siblings living in the same house. She lived with her grandmother about eight years. Sadly, her loving grandmother died in a horrific car accident on the way to kidney dialysis treatment.

After Niki's grandmother died conditions changed again for Nakita. This time another aunt became her guardian with the help of other family members. Some may see this as another setback and interference with Niki's education, however, I term it "Divine Intervention." She was assigned to a different elementary school in the school district and her life was never the same again, in Jesus' name!

Intermediate Education

Through "Divine Intervention," a new fourth grader by the name of Nakita Taylor was assigned to my fourth grade class. Her life would never be the same, in Jesus' name! You may think that is a little arrogant on my part but you must understand that God had already prepared me for this precious miraculous child. She was nine years old and had the most beautiful smile you have ever seen, but with all the conditions stated earlier. I thought it was ironic that I was assigned Niki because I had attended high school with both aunts. The second aunt was a classmate of mine when I first entered high school. She knew that Niki was in good hands with me as her teacher.

I feel that it is imperative that I share my philosophy of education with you so you can grasp the statement about why I felt that God had already prepared me for Niki. I firmly believe that education is the key to success. With this belief foremost in my mind, all my energy is devoted to making learning both challenging and exciting. It is extremely important how children feel about themselves in their environment.

High on my list of priorities is helping children develop a strong self-concept. Guiding children through successful experiences seem to spark their enthusiasm for increased learning. Self-motivation can generate desired behaviors. This motivational inquiry demonstrates academic freedom to excel beyond one's imagination. Learning of this kind is exemplary of supervisory dedication. As an educator, one must prepare children to become productive, responsible citizens. To this end, educators must pursue all avenues that will enhance the learning ability of all children. This objective can be achieved by keeping abreast of changes in education, learning new strategies, and applying those strategies to the individual differences of children.

There were many opportunities for Niki to thrive and grow in my class and that is just what she did! One vivid example of noticeable change in Niki's confidence was when I was teaching the students the Scientific Method in preparation for a science fair at our school. This lesson sparked enthusiasm in Nakita to explain why she drooled, spoke with a slur, walked with a limp, and held her hand a certain way. It was as if a light bulb had been turned on in her head. She shared her idea with me and obtained permission from her aunt to do the project.

The project was entitled "The Effects of Drugs on Babies." I knew this project could not be tested using the scientific method, but I allowed her to do it knowing it would help her understand what happened to her before she was born. Talking about her disability helped her to heal and gave her the opportunity to testify to God's goodness and the miraculous work he had performed in her life. It was simply her way of telling her own story and she has been telling it ever since that magical day! The project even won an honorable mention in the school's science fair.

The most moving moment at the fair was when one of the school board members wept after reading her story. The scenario was captured in the local paper the following day. Niki's life has never been the same, in Jesus' name. She had finally found an avenue to help her heal.

Middle School

The middle school years were especially cruel to Nakita. She described it as part of the "Years from Hell." As you know, peers are most important to preteen students at this vulnerable time. Being socially acceptable is a high priority for many of them. Reflect back to this adolescent girl with partial Cerebral Palsy, walking with a limp, slurred speech, and drooling. These differences made Niki a prime candidate for her peers to harass her unmercifully on a daily basis. She had no friends and saw herself as an embarrassment to the world and constantly questioned how life would be if she did not have these disabilities. She fantasized about having many friends, and how she would be unafraid of approaching others.

However, when she shook herself back to reality, her own body testified against her. There was a heinous group of girls who teased and called her all sorts of names. Everywhere she went they would follow her and imitate her disability. It was so bad that she felt her little heart had been ripped into tiny pieces. She really could not understand because she tried so hard to fit in, but the abuse just continued. At lunch, Niki drooled when she ate and the kids made fun of her. Therefore, most of the time, she ate alone so she would not have to communicate with anyone. In Niki's mind, "Silence Is Golden" resonated to the core of her being. One would think that these girls would just stop taunting Niki, but it got worse.

Niki became so angry that she finally had to let it all out! She just could not deal with it anymore. In a rage, she said to these girls, "If you don't stop teasing me I am going into the school's kitchen and get a knife and cut you into small pieces." She really did not mean this but she thought these girls would leave her alone. It did not happen. The next day they followed her to her locker in the hallway and continued to tease her, and as she walked away, they laughed aloud. They also mad fun of her in class when the teacher would call upon her. From that point on, she would just stare off into space. Finally, she could not take the teasing anymore so she went to her aunts and burst into tears. She had taken it long enough.

The next day one of her aunts visited the school and talked to the counselor about the ordeal. The counselor addressed the issue with the girls, but they just called her stupid and said she could not defend herself. They also said they wanted to "kick her butt." Surely, you can see why Niki described her middle school years as part of her "Years from Hell."

High School

The flames of Hell burned profusely and it was much the same as middle school. The only difference was that Niki was getting older and the heated insults were becoming more intense. Nikita hated school. This was the time in her life when she was supposed to spend time with friends and do fun things together. It was also the time one should fall in love, go on dates, to dances, and see the latest movies. She knew the script, but it just did not happen that way. It only happened like that in the movies.

In reality, Niki faked happiness. She did not want to go to the school dances and only went to make her aunt think that she was happy. Niki had a very low self-esteem and became good at hiding her feelings. She never wanted to be a burden to anyone. Therefore, she kept going to school functions, including the dances, even though she knew nobody wanted to dance with her. After each function, she would go home and say that she had a good time. Nevertheless, each night she would cry herself to sleep. The Lord was her only comforter and protector.

The one thing that kept her going was speaking engagements. These activities took place outside the school. When you peer into Niki's scrapbook, you will find a precious picture of a princess who grew into a queen in her community. She continues to evolve as she accomplishes more of her personal goals. I truly believe that God has preserved her for such a time as this. Since ten years of age, Niki has spoke to many audiences of both children and adults. Her first speech was at Beachland Elementary.

Some years following her debut at the science fair, I attended a Children's Summit, and as fate would have it, or what I term "Divine Intervention," I met a retired nurse who was a leading advocate for a *Drug Free America*. At some point, she had cut out an article from the local newspaper about Niki and kept it. She recognized me as Niki's teacher at the summit. The headline read "Girl Uses Own History to Teach Against Drugs." She also fell in love with this young woman and her message to bring about change in the hope that no other baby would ever endure what she experienced. This nurse and I formed a bond and a platform providing Niki opportunities that will extend the reach of her voice in articulating her story.

Rotary International, through its annual Youth Leadership Program, helped Niki gain confidence in herself by providing leadership skills and sponsored her to various conferences where she also spoke. Later, the local Rotary Club provided her with a scholarship to attend a week long National Leadership Conference in Rhode Island. This was a *Youth to Youth* conference with the theme: Drug Free by Design. Niki shared her fourth grade science project on babies and drugs. To this end, Niki has shared the podium with some well renowned speakers. One of the most prominent speakers she shared the stage with was Dr. Andrea Barthwell, Deputy Director for Demand Reduction for the White House Office of National Drug Policy under President George W. Bush.

Another community service program Niki works tirelessly with is the Science Institute of Discovery, Inc. In this nonprofit program, she assists in leadership with its founder in helping underprivileged students in the district learn more about science through hands-on experiences.

All of these extracurricular activities helped prevent Niki from dropping out of school and becoming more depressed. She graduated with her class in spite of the fact that she termed her secondary school experience as being some of the "Years from Hell!"

Post Secondary Education

Niki continued her speaking engagements and went on to receive many accolades. She won local, district, and state awards.

Today, Nikita attends Indian River Community College on a full scholarship afforded her by a special husband and wife team. This was a family sent from Heaven. Only God could plant a seed of compassion into the hearts of individuals such as these folks.

Words of the Writer

Early one morning, toward the dawn of a new year while on my fitness run, my journey allowed me to capture through my peripheral vision an amazing architectural web of a spider. The spider had no inclination that I was peering into its wonders and being mesmerized by its divine order to orchestrate such a magnificent structure. It was revealing to me at this time that I should attempt to tell Nakita's story from this premise.

It became very clear to me that God was the nucleus, the giver of life from Heaven. Everyone and everything else were external factors with which His precious gift, called Nakita Sherrell Taylor, entangled with as she journeyed through this web called life. I am still haunted by these profound questions:

"Who is caught up in whose web?"

"Is it the observer or the observed?"

Gary Hagen

was born in Ft. Belvoir, VA and spent most of his life in California. He relocated to historical Mt. Dora, FL, where he opened the Hollywood Cheese Cake Café. He later changed the name to the House of David Upper Room Café.

Gary is a culinary master having owned eight restaurants. He has served Clint Eastwood, Jimmy Stewart, Doris Day, Kim Novak, Secretary of State Shultz, and many other celebrities. Gary has worked in the restaurant business for 35 years, well known for his famous cheesecakes.

He has served on the staff of Joyce Meyers Ministries. He is affectionately called the "Cheesecake Man," having made 500 cheesecakes for her staff. Gary worked as a volunteer for Joyce Meyers Dream Center and Genesis Group Men's Ministry; both programs centered on the needs of inner city individuals and were part of her prison and inner city ministry during the two years he lived in St. Louis, MO. He is a past member of the Culinary Academy of Culinary Professionals and served his country in the Marine Corp. Gary received a Citizen Service Citation from the St Louis County Police Department for an act of heroism.

Contact information: cheesecakegary@yahoo.com

A Voice in the Dark

Gary woke suddenly from a sound sleep. "What was that?" His foggy brain tried to identify the sounds that seemed to be coming from somewhere outside his window. "It could be the neighbor's kids coming home," he decided. As his head cleared, the noises became more vivid and he suddenly realized he was actually hearing screams. His mind flashed back to earlier that night. He had seen a man prowling around his neighbor's house and called the police. The prowler had disappeared before any of the officers arrived. Gary asked the police to patrol the neighborhood frequently to prevent the man from coming back. Now, his mind nearly exploded with alarm!

Gary leaped from his bed, grabbing a pair of long pants, and hopped across the room as he hurriedly pulled them on. He raced to the front door, flung it open, stuck his head out, and listened. His hair nearly stood on end as the most terrifying scream he had ever heard pierced the night air. He groped wildly, while trying to find his phone in the pitch-black room. "911, is this a police, medical, or fire emergency?" "I need the police right away. I called you earlier tonight, now he is in the neighbor's house. I can hear her screaming!" "Calm down, sir. I will dispatch a unit to your location immediately. Just stay put and wait for the police to arrive." "Thanks, please tell them to hurry," he pleaded.

Throughout his call to 911 the screams continued, followed by several thuds. Images of his neighbor shot through his mind. She was only twenty-five and he knew her boyfriend was out of town. She was alone with no one to help her. As the screams grew louder, he raced towards his front door. "I've got to do something. The police may not get here in time. She needs my help! God, what should I do?" He frantically began looking for a weapon while he passed through the living room. "You don't need a weapon." These firm reassuring words filled his mind.

Gary ran out the front door without a weapon and began to cross his front porch when he suddenly heard a voice say, "You need to go and put on your heaviest sweater because he's going to try to bite you." "O.k., if you say so," he mumbled as he turned back towards his house. Running to his bedroom, he threw on a thick, black sweater. Suddenly, the screams stopped. This frightened him even more. As he raced back

Multiple Streams of Success

outside, the piercing screams began again. It felt like they were going right through him. Tears streamed down his face.

Suddenly, everything became silent. "Oh no, I don't hear her anymore. I hope she is still alive. What can I do? God, help me!" He quietly stood at the back door of his neighbor's home for a moment, listening intently for any clues as to what might be happening inside. He heard a man talking, but there was no response from his neighbor. Then, he frantically threw himself against the kitchen door several times until the lock broke. Then, he walked into the room.

"Just relax. It will be over in a few minutes," came a voice from somewhere in the room. As Gary's eyes struggled to see in the dim light, he was able to make out the form of his neighbor, Lisa, face down on the floor. A man was on top of her with his hands around her throat.

Looking up, the man saw Gary and calmly said, "What are you doing here? You do not need to be here. Just leave."

"What are you doing? Are you nuts?" Gary replied.

The man slowly got up, began walking towards Gary, who noticed that the neighbor still was not moving, and feared he had not gotten there soon enough.

"I've got to get out of here!" the man exclaimed.

"You're not leaving. You're not getting out of here," countered Gary. The guy began moving back and forth; trying to reach the door to escape, but Gary blocked him.

Suddenly, the man took off towards the bathroom, where there was a hallway leading out to the living room. Gary knew if the intruder made it to the living room, he would be able to get out the front door and could escape into the woods. Racing from a hallway that led from the other side of the kitchen Gary was able to cut the guy off and caught him in a bear hug to subdue him. "Let me go. Let me go," were his frantic protests.

The next sounds he heard were music to his ears, "Oh God, Gary! Oh God, Gary! Oh God, Gary! Thank God, Gary! Thank God, Gary!" The grateful cries seemed to spur the attacker on. He struggled wildly to get away and Gary slammed him against the wall to calm him down. He did not want the man anywhere near Lisa.

The wrestling match had been going on for ten to fifteen minutes when the room was illuminated by revolving lights from several police cars. The man became more violent and began biting Gary on his arm, hands, and finally his chest, as he frantically tried to get away. The attacker bit through the bulky sweater into flesh of Gary chest. The intense struggle continued until Gary threw the man onto a chair and held him down so the police could handcuff him.

When the police burst into the room Gary lifted up his free hand saying, "I'm the good guy. I'm the good guy. I'm John Wayne!" He did not want to take any chances of getting shot or tased. He started to release the intruder to the police so they could handcuff him. With an extreme burst of energy, the guy got away.

Gary lunged toward the attacker and grabbed the back of his shirt. It slowly ripped from his body. Gary saw this entire scene evolve like it was in slow motion. This delayed him slightly as he passed through the doorway. Outside, several police officers apprehended the crazed attacker, Dale McKenzie, and put him into a squad car.

Relief flooded through Gary, as he turned away and began to look for his neighbor. He found her standing on the steps outside the kitchen door. She burst into tears when she saw him and he noticed that she was shaking violently.

"He was trying to kill me!" she sobbed hysterically.

"It's all right now. They caught the guy and he can't hurt you anymore." He hugged Lisa and walked her out towards her car, thinking it would be better to put some space between themselves and the crime scene.

Soon, the police came over to question them. An ambulance arrived and took Lisa to the hospital for an examination. Gary followed the ambulance to the emergency room in his car. Somehow, the nurses thought he was the man who had attacked Lisa and treated him roughly for a while. Gary felt quite uncomfortable, especially since they put Lisa in a room down the hall and he did not get to see her for several hours. He hoped and prayed that she would be okay, both physically and emotionally.

A nurse finally led him down the hall to the room where Lisa was lying. "Gary, thank you so much

Multiple Streams of Success

for coming over to help me. You saved my life! I'm so grateful!"

"I'm just glad the guy who broke in is behind bars and you're safe now," he responded with a sigh of relief.

During the next three days, Gary was filled with a wonderful sense of peace and the presence of God. He was able to minister to Lisa's entire family in a powerful way. He had never done anything like that before. Looking back, he sees those days as a time of training, where he learned to minister to those who were hurting.

The story of Gary's bravery was in newspapers and he learned that McKenzie was an ex-convict wanted in eight states for murder and rape. The St. Louis Board of Police Commissioners gave Gary a beautiful, framed Citizen Service Citation. The citation commended him for his bravery and decisive action, which prevented any further injury, probably saved his neighbor's life, and resulted in the arrest of a violent convicted sex offender. The attacker was eventually sentenced to life imprisonment, plus 31 years, which means he will never be released.

This experience was a turning point for Gary. Through it, he learned to hear God's voice. This took Gary to a entirely new dimension and created a better understanding of whom God really is and who he is in Christ.

Gary now says, "Many people promise they'll do things for God, but give up when things get a little tough. God revealed that he had chosen me to help my neighbor and there is nothing I will not do for God. I learned that I am willing to stand up and do what is needed, without fear. To risk my life for another is one of the most powerful things I've ever experienced."

Lisa has kept in touch with Gary. She moved to another state in 2007 and married. On March 1, 2008, she became the mother of a beautiful baby girl. Gary remains moved to tears when he thinks of how God empowered him and used him to stand up, without fear, against evil. He experienced, firsthand, that "With God all things are possible."

The House of David Upper Room Café

Gary is now involved, by the grace of God, in a ministry restaurant named the House of David Upper Room Café, where as he says "we walk in faith with no prices on the menu." Many people have asked, "Why?" His answer is always the same, "I believe in what the spirit of God shares with me. I am a strong believer in faith. By removing the prices, only accepting donations, and having no money in the cash drawer, is a physical manifestation of faith. I simply allow God to fill the drawer. Nestled in the heart of historic Mt. Dora, FL, we have touched the lives of thousands of people, locally and around the world."

Gary believes he is a living testimony of adversities overcome through faith resulting in powerfully successful outcomes that impact those around him.

Pam Rodgers

is an Inspirational Speaker, a Certified Dream Coach, CEO & Founder Dream-ALot non-profit foundation, and a Realtor™.

Pam Rodgers has inspired thousands of children and adults in both the US and internationally on "Living an Inspired Life." She will coach you to find your purpose in life, identify what you ultimately want out of life and strategies on how to achieve it. She delivers a high-energy, thought provoking, life-changing message that lights up the human spirit. The transformation of human lives is captivating!

Accolades include BS SJSU Corporate Health Promotion & Stress Management, Trail Blazer Award ARAMARK Sports and Entertainment, Realtor™ of the Year 2007 Intero Real Estate Services, North County Monterey High School Keynote Speaker, Intero Real Estate Coach, and Trainer "Living an Inspired Life."

Contact Information: prodgers@interorealestate.com

A Conversation with God!

Is this all there is?

Okay God, I know you did not bring me this far to have it end like this. It is November 11, 2005 at 11:30 am and I find myself in a hospital gown sitting in a small room at the Cancer Treatment Center in San Jose, Ca. The room is small with six chairs against the walls and three small changing rooms. I come in upbeat and bubbly as I usually do, change into my gown and sit waiting to be called for my turn to have my radiation treatment. I look around the room and make small talk with the other women who are also in hospital gowns.

I am usually the upbeat positive one with the glass half-full and always something positive to say. Today it seems difficult to find positive words for others while I am worried about myself and what having cancer is going to mean for my life.

I sit quietly looking around the room at the faces of the other women and wonder who sitting here is going to live and who is going to die? It seems so profound to know that statistically some of us in this room will die from cancer in the next few months or years and wondering which of us it will be.

I then look into the eyes of a daughter who came to support her Mom. I can feel the daughters fear and uncertainty. Her Mom is young, probably only late forties, and is full of life and hope.

I ask the usual question… "What are you here for?" It seems so silly to ask that way, but the word cancer is hard to say. What we are really asking each other is what type of cancer do you have and what is your prognosis? What we are really asking each other is "Are you going to die?"

This amazing woman turns to me and says with grace that her cancer is in her brain and several internal organs. As she says it, you can tell she "believes" she is going to beat this thing. As I look at her, I am equally as confident by her prognosis that she will die soon and wonder how her daughter will survive losing her Mom. I have to turn my eyes away because I start to cry and I do not want anyone to see. The room is closing in on me. I feel a desperate need to leave but I am wearing this darn hospital gown, and there is nowhere to go. I am telling myself inside to "suck it up" and "don't you dare let them see you cry!" In addition, whatever you do, do not tell them why you are crying. You see it was only fourteen months earlier that I was the daughter taking

Multiple Streams of Success

my Mom to the Cancer treatment center for her radiation treatment. I would push her into the building stoic and full of hope and smiling at every doctor and patient with this look that My Mom is going to make it. My Mom died at home on August 16, 2004 of lung cancer.

Let me tell you a little about my Mom. She was an amazing woman, full of energy, spirit, compassion, and most of all adventure. She flew small airplanes, taught me how to fish, and built a kit car in the garage with a friend of hers. She drove around as often as possible in a little MG convertible with the top down. She lived a very big life. I remember playing soccer at college and Mom would fly up to see the games but before she would land, she would "buzz" the field to say hello first. My teammates would say, hey what is that plane doing so low and waving their wings? Are they in trouble? I would say "no worries. That's just my Mom, as I would stare and wave beaming up at the sky." My Mom was full of life and lived life fully!

Around April of 2001, Mom went in for open-heart surgery. She was getting a new valve. When they were prepping her for surgery, they did an MRI that showed a spot on her lung that raised some concern.

They needed to do a biopsy to see what it was. In Rodgers fashion my Mom said "Can't you have the pulmonary doctor there while my chest is opened-up to do the biopsy?" The doctor thought she was crazy and said, "Open-heart surgery is major surgery and the cardiac doctor will not want to leave you opened up waiting for another doctor to work on you." My Mom was persuasive and said, "You may as well do it all at once and save us all some time." Therefore, they did. Unfortunately, when she came out of the open-heart surgery we had the results back from the lung biopsy and she awoke to find out she had lung cancer.

The next three years were a whirlwind. Mom recovered from her open-heart surgery and we slipped into a healthy level of denial regarding her cancer. I do remember the first day I took Mom to the Oncologist to find out what all this meant. He was describing the cancer, the symptoms, and what to expect. He used all sorts of technical names, but all I heard was that it was inoperable and slow growing. I then looked at him and asked "the question we all want to know (all except my Mom), what does slow growing mean? Are we talking years or decades?" In my mind, slow growing could mean twenty or thirty years for the tumor to reach a

40

critical size. At some level, I think we all want to know how much time we have on this planet so we know how to plan our life.

I remember so vividly as if it was yesterday when he said maybe two to three years. I immediately lost my breath as if the wind was knocked out of me. I tried to hold back the tears but it was nearly impossible. I started to count the number of Christmas's we would have and tried to put into context in my brain what two years looked like.

Later, Mom shared with me that she wished I had not asked "that" question because she would have rather not known. On some level, we all know we can die any day and should not take people or time for granted, but it sure is different when you have a ticking clock handed to you with a finite amount of time. It changes EVERYTHING!

I remember sitting with Mom at lunch that day wondering what we should do, where should we go, how should I act with her knowing she has two years left. Do I quit my job and spend every moment with her? She certainly did not want that. What I learned from that moment is that every moment we spend with someone may be the last and we had better show up, be present, and enjoy it because none of us knows how much time we have. It made the simple things seem much more important like talking over dinner, watching Jeopardy, having a Starbucks and reading the paper together. I listened more intently to her stories about life, her relatives, her first jobs, and meeting my Dad. I hung on every word. I wondered why I did not listen this well last month or last year. I wanted her to repeat all her stories. She was a great storyteller and could remember ALL the details, dates, names, places. I wanted ALL of that now. I became like a sponge to learn all I could. I made more time for dinner dates instead of working late.

In April of 2004, Mom started becoming noticeably short of breath. She played it off as if it was nothing. I knew better. We did not talk about it anymore, but we all knew she was in the process of dying. It had been three years and we were now on borrowed time. The next four months were incredibly hard. Mom got progressively sicker and began her radiation treatment. The doctors said that the radiation treatment would help with the pain but would not cure the cancer.

Mom still held to her story that she was going to beat this thing. It took everything out of her to get to radiation. We had to drug her with morphine because the pain was so excruciating just to get her into the car. Some days I wondered why we were going since it was not going to help but Mom believed she was going to beat this thing and this was one of the steps to do it.

The week Mom died was the Tour de' France and Lance Armstrong was winning. Mom was sitting on the edge of her bed with her yellow "Live Strong" bracelet on cheering aloud for Lance. I believe on some level she thought if he could beat it, so could she. She was really cheering for the power of the human spirit. I think Lance represented for Mom, and still does for so many of us, the power of the human spirit. That no matter what life throws at you, and how impossible it seems, that through hard work and BELIEVING the human spirit can overcome anything! Mom lost her fight to cancer on August 16, 2004, but she never stopped believing. She never stopped living for one moment.

The year after my Mom died was incredibly difficult, but for reasons I had not anticipated. My Mom was my very best friend, as well as my mentor, my marriage counselor, my financial advisor, my coach, and so much more. My Mom was very vocal, acknowledging how proud she was of my four sisters and me. No matter what we did, Mom was always there.

Without her cheering for me, life took on an emptiness that was gut wrenching. I went to work. I hung out with friends. I continued to do the things I previously did, but there was an indescribable void. I used to speak to Mom everyday. Now when something great would happen and I picked up the phone to call I realized there was no one to call. It certainly took the joy out of many of the things I did without Mom to celebrate. I was on my own. No one to share great things with and no one to look to for help, support or that invisible net that we know is there if we fall. It is not that I ever needed it, but it sure was nice to know it was there.

My Dad died when I was seventeen years old. He was fifty years old and committed suicide. He gassed himself in the car in our garage. My younger sister, who was fifteen at the time, was the one who found him. She tried to resuscitate him but was unable. He died on September 20, 1980. It seems somewhat bizarre, but we all managed. We picked ourselves up by our bootstraps and moved on. Just like, we were taught. I now recognize it as hard-core denial, but I guess it served us well at the time. We did not even talk about it much. I guess I coped by numbing out.

I had been using drugs recreationally since I was ten years old. I have three older sisters and I guess I bugged them enough to let me join them one day and the rest is history. They stopped using drugs and I proceeded to fine-tune my drug use for many years to come. All through elementary school and high school, I managed to continue to get good grades, play sports, and be a role model for many. After my father died, however my drug use escalated.

For the next eight years, my life proceeded to fall apart. I could not hold a job; I was dropping out of classes in college and losing myself spiritually and emotionally. I was using cocaine to wake up and marijuana to calm down. I drank alcohol to balance it all out. It was only by God's grace that I finished school and managed to get good grades. As I think back on it, God was with me long before I ever turned to him. I never got a DUI, arrested, or physically injured using drugs and alcohol. God's grace is amazing to me.

As a child I was raised Catholic but could not relate to the formality of the Catholic Church so at age sixteen was re-baptized in a non-denominational church. It was here I learned about having a relationship with

God. This changed my life forever; I just would not realize it for many years to come.

In the spring of 1987, I found myself heavily addicted to crack cocaine, seriously malnourished and working as a food server only so I could steal enough money to support my drug habit. I could barely leave my home because of the drug-induced paranoia. I was absolutely at a bottom and wanted to take my life. The pain I felt from losing my father and reality of the permanency of suicide was the only thing that kept me from taking my own life. Instead, I desperately reached out to my family for help. I checked into a thirty-day in-patient treatment center in Mountain View, CA. I wish I could say it ended there but I relapsed twice after getting out of treatment.

The truth is I am an addict through and through. I learned to respect the power of my addiction and my disease and that I am not safe using anything mind altering. Moderation is not something I have mastered in my life and so I choose my addictions very carefully and do not put myself in situations that can jeopardize my recovery.

Moderation in other areas of my life is something I am working on. Some sense of balance would serve me in areas such as money, fitness, diet, and overcoming perfectionism. What I have learned is to understand the value of humility, trusting in my relationship with God and letting go. I am happy to say that today I am celebrating eighteen years clean and sober and practice a twelve-step program of recovery.

Let us to back to being in the cancer treatment center in my hospital gown. I wish I could tell you I got my answers all at once. Well God did not reveal it to me that way; he fed it to me in pieces.

My conversation with God started one day while I was lying on the radiation table, in the same position I imagine my Mom had laid. I was wondering if I was going to die, too. I asked God quietly that day what plans he had for me. "God, I know you did not bring me through all of this in my life to let me die now. I also know that you always use people and situations for good. What good do you have planned for me Lord? Is my usefulness to you going to come in the form of my death or my living?" I started to ask if my life actually had served anyone and what would people say about me at my funeral. "Lord, are you there? What would people say about me? Have I served you well, Lord? Has my life had purpose? I am not sure what my purpose is Lord... so how do I know if I have served it?"

My journey started that day, still not knowing if I would live or die but knowing that my time might be very short, to ensure I had lived a purposeful life. What now, God?

It was a crisp sunny afternoon in January and I went on a walk in the mountains near my house right above the Gates of Heaven Cemetery where my parents were buried. It is somewhat funny actually, every time I asked God for an answer he threw it back at me. I asked what is my life suppose to be about? He asked me, "What do you want it to be about?"

"What will people say about me if I die?" I would ask. "What do you want people to say about you?"

"What should I do with my life if I live and survive cancer?" He said, "What do you want to do with your life?"

He whispered the questions gently, compassionately, and with encouragement directly to my soul as if God and my mom were both talking to me.

It was on this day that I reflected back on my upbringing and thought, "WOW... my folks have always raised me to believe I could do anything and be anything." As a family of five girls, if one of us wanted to play on the boys' basketball team they would say "join the boys' team or start your own team." They never said we could not! They never discouraged. They never said, "Be practical or realistic." Therefore, I decided to try this on for size and see if I could tap into that… what would I do if I could do or be anything.

What makes me happiest? I began to think about the human spirit and how lucky I was to have my particular set of parents and for being reared in that specific family and environment. A family that did not limit beliefs and a family where I could be anything, go anywhere, or do anything. That is powerful! Too bad, it took me getting cancer to remember these amazing words of wisdom. I began thinking about stories of people that have overcome great challenges. Moreover, I began to wonder why some people make it out from a burning airplane or from being trapped on a mountain and other people lie down and die. What separates these people? What makes them different?

The walk up the mountain that day changed my life forever because it connected me with my heart and my soul. The walk got me to ask myself some deep questions about who I am and what I wanted out of my life. Whether I have a long time or a short time on this planet, what do I want my life to stand for? Over the next few months, I had an opportunity to re-script my life, one without limiting beliefs. Here is what I decided...

I wanted to change my career. I really liked my job a lot but it was not filling my soul or serving my life purpose. My life purpose was to inspire people to live their dreams. To be the champion of the human spirit to encourage and dream with you as my parents did and allowed me to do. I knew I would go into real estate as my next career, but I was afraid of giving up a salary and benefits. When I prayed about this, God answered back with "walk in faith and I will not let you fail." Nevertheless, there was so much more I wanted to do in addition to a new career.

On April 6, 2006, just sixteen months after losing my Mom to cancer and just six months from hearing I had breast cancer; I resigned from my job and left with these words: "I have to go change the world."

I was not sure how it was going to happen but I knew I had to try. God told me not to worry I don't have to change it all at once, I could do it one person at a time, like a pebble thrown into a pond and the ripples it sends out. If I can help, serve, or inspire one person at a time, he or she will in turn go help one other person who will help one other person and on and on. Indeed, in that way, I believe I can change the world and live my life's purpose.

In the twelve months since leaving my job, I obtained my real estate license and I am helping others to pursue their dreams through investing in real estate. So much for the fear about money, I doubled my income in the first year and the change of career has allowed me the opportunity to pursue my passion and desire to give back.

My partner and I founded a 501(c)(3) non-profit foundation named Dream-ALot. The foundation is working towards building an inspirational camp fondly named CAMP CAMELOT "Where impossible dreams come true" to open May 2011. The camp will serve to inspire both children and adults to live an extraordinary life. At its core, Camp Camelot is about inspiring people to live their dreams. When human beings' souls awaken to what is POSSIBLE, and they BELIEVE, magic happens!

Magic has certainly happened for me. Cancer stripped away the fear I had and replaced it with faith; the faith in God to guide me and the courage to take steps to make magic happen. I am now giving inspirational speeches all over the world helping others to find their purpose and the courage to pursue their dreams. I am writing a book to help people identify priorities in their life so they can spend more time on creating joy. I am clean, sober, and cancer free! Cancer turned out to be a blessing for me and now I talk to God all the time… and I still ask him, "Is this all there is? God, how can I serve you today? What will they say about me when I die?"

Don Sepulveda

is President of Sepulveda Insurance Group, which was recently named as one of the "Ten Most Dependable Agencies in the Eastern United States." Forbes Magazine published the announcement of this prestigious honor. His company provides thousands of jobs and serves thousands of clients throughout the United States. He gives sales and motivational training to countless agents.

Don is living proof that you do not have to allow your past, no matter how negative it might have been, to dictate your future. Following a childhood fraught with extreme mental and physical abuse and being abandoned in his early teens, Don was determined to make a better life in the future for himself, and for anyone with whom his life paths would cross. While building a multi-million dollar a year Insurance Agency Don also works as a country and Christian music recording Artist. He has charted over 20 records on country radio, won first place in Ed McMahon's "Next Big Star" competition, and continues to achieve successes typically only attained by full-time musicians. He has appeared on television, on the Grand Ole Opry stage, professionally recorded and performed his music in many venues yet still maintains determination to keep his family at the top of his life's priorities.

Don considers himself very blessed for the opportunity to achieve simultaneous success in two completely opposite professions, both of which are difficult and complex industries.

Don is a long time member in his Church Praise Band, and enjoys participating in Golf, Karate, custom motorcycles, and music. He lives in Cumming, Georgia with his wife Nora, and their daughters Candice and Donna. Their oldest daughter, Tabitha, is married, and has added two grandchildren, Alexis and Austin, to the family.

Contact information: don@sepulvedainsurance.com

A Mother's Wounds
A Child's Anguish
God's Grace

I was born on my mother's birthday, June 2. Sadly, she was a mere child herself, turning just fifteen years of age on that day and yet, I was not her first child. I had a sister, eleven months older than I was. These statistics would prove devastating to many people in countless ways. My real father would leave within a month or two and, although he lived only twenty minutes away, I would not know him until meeting him at my sister's funeral 17 years later.

I would not be able to understand until much later in life the reasons for some of the terrible things that went on behind the doors of our "seemingly" normal middle class house, and for some of the darkest secrets we may never find real closure. Our mother denied all requests to talk about the past as we got old enough to want answers for what had happened to us, and why. Her response was always, "It's in the past, and you really don't want to know." She was wrong. We *really did* want to know. Actually, we **needed** to know.

However, she died one Christmas morning and took with her the truth we needed to hear.

I refer to "we" in this text because, in one of the most painful revelations in my life, I discovered that one of my younger sisters had endured some of the same abuses that I did. Although we were in the same house, I was not aware of my little sister's suffering. That fact still causes me deep sadness. I so wish I could have been there to help her in some way even though we were so young. Perhaps at least to share the experience of physical and emotional pain inflicted upon us might have made it more bearable, I do not really know. I do know that, for some strange reason, it created a deeper sorrow to learn that she had been through some of these tribulations than the feelings I felt for myself.

Much memory of my early years is blocked in a way I cannot describe. Our brains have a wonderful and powerful ability to protect us from things we cannot emotionally handle. One of my few remaining memories of early life at home is of being called to the kitchen by my mother while she was preparing hot tea, which was not unusual. Except this time when I went to her as she had told me to do, she took the pan of boiling water from the burner and poured it on me. Words fail me in attempting to describe the intensity of the pain I felt that day. Yet, aside from the burns I had suffered, there was a deeper wound inflicted that day which hurt much worse and lasted infinitely longer. There was laughter coming from my mother as the skin on my right shoulder and upper arm literally separated from my body and began to fall off. I ran screaming to the shower to do the only thing I could think of, to stand under the cold water in a desperate attempt to ease the burning and absorb the shock of what had just happened.

Our mother was a unique woman with a strikingly attractive appearance that cloaked a very disturbed and powerful personality. She was from a wealthy family that was able to give her whatever she wanted, with the exception of love and attention.

Her beauty enabled her to effortlessly attract many men into her life. While I do not remember all of the men who came and left, I do know that Mom had a habit of consistently choosing men that were laden with their own sets of serious problems. This trait would serve to multiply the variations of abusive behaviors to which we were subjected.

I never knew why my mother felt a need to make me stand at attention facing the wall, sometimes for days at a time. The mental and physical fatigue was literally torture to me, especially as I heard other people in the house carrying on, eating, watching T.V. etc. I would count breaths, heartbeats, seconds, or anything I could do to help pass the time including using my imagination to create images in the texture of the paint on the wall.

One day as I stood in my usual spot, no one was in the house except Mom and me. She came to me and placed a gun to the side of my head. Without any comment, she held that position for what seemed an eternity as I fully expected to hear the explosion of gunfire at any second. I wondered how this was going to feel and how long would the pain of the experience last? Finally, she asked me if I knew why she was not pulling the trigger. I do not have enough memory of what happened next to provide accurate details.

Many times, I would watch neighborhood children playing outside. I had to stand tiptoe on the toilet seat and strain to see outside through the high window of the bathroom in which I was locked. The doorknobs were turned backwards so the locks would work from the outside of the door. I have never forgotten the feelings of longing to be out there with those children, unrestrained and free to enjoy the splendor of the wondrous outdoors. They seemed so happy.

Meals during this period would consist of a bowl containing a mixture of bread, milk, and sugar. I found creative ways to hide, and later discard or flush this disgusting concoction, until I became too hungry to care any more. I don't know what my sister did with hers, but, as I have only recently been made aware, she was locked in her room and was being forced to eat the same "meal" that I was being given.

There were always "step fathers" in and out of our house. Mom was married many times. I truly do not know the actual number of marriages, but suffice it to say it was at least ten. There was abuse from some of these men, as well. I cannot even remember the faces or names of many of them. None of them ever lifted a finger to stop Mom from giving me the beatings, endless lock-ins, food deprivation, methods of alienation and seclusion, force-feeding spoons full of Cheyenne pepper, verbal and physical abuse, and much more.

I longed for a "hero" to come along who would stand up to this frightening woman and save me from this life of constant fear. No one did. There came a day when my mother told me we were going for a ride. I had no idea that we were headed for a place called Juvenile Hall until we drove up to a large building with all of the appearances of a prison.

They checked me in and took me down a long hallway where they put me in a small cement block room. One memory I have not been able to block from my mind, even though I would like to, is the sound of the heavy steel door slamming shut and the man walking away leaving me alone to wonder how a mother could have so much hate for her own child.

In addition, where was God through all of this?

This was absolutely the loneliest and most frightening time I had ever experienced even considering the long term "lock-ins" I had been through at home. Why had every person abandoned me and why were my pleas to God for help going unheard?

Finally, His answer came. One day a man said something to me that I have never forgotten. He told me I did not belong in that place. I could tell he meant it in a good way and I was so unaccustomed to hearing anything positive said to me that it took time to register in my mind. Those few words meant so much to me. He apparently had me released from Juvenile Hall and I was placed in a foster wait center.

I have no concept of the amount of time spent there, but I saw other kids come and go. It was a better place in many ways than where I had been. We were not locked in tiny cold rooms, we could watch TV, go outside, and not live as prisoners, but this place introduced a new set of challenges. Still, it was a big improvement, for which I was grateful.

I cannot recall what happened from there. I never knew my real father until we met at my older sister's funeral. She died on her eighteenth birthday. I was seventeen. Here was the man that shared my name. He seemed like a good man. I could tell he really loved Shirley and her death was devastating to him. I just wished I could have known him years earlier. I know things could have been very different. We now live three thousand miles apart and rarely see one another.

At the time of this writing, he has never been to my home. I am not sure he truly knows anything about how my family and I live our lives. Never before have I had the occasion to write about these issues in this way. I thank you for allowing me to share these things. There is so much more to say, but limited space will not allow me to continue. Now to quote Paul Harvey, let me give you "the *rest* of the story."

I must admit to you, I have wallowed in long periods of self-pity. Poor me! Why has God abandoned me? What could I have done that was bad enough to deserve this kind of life? Where were the men who were supposed to be "fathers" while all of this was happening and so on?

I wish I had more room to tell you about several major life events that reshaped my thinking and helped me realize that **I am not one to be pitied.** <u>I have come to believe that some of us must endure things for the sake of others</u>. Everything we go through makes us who we are. Every painful thing that happened to me as a child contributed to my determination ultimately to do something meaningful with my life, and to be very sensitive to the needs and feelings of others.

The personality traits that developed in me eventually created success in my life in unexpected ways. Please know that I am nowhere near where I need to be, but I am a long way from where I started. I am grateful for that. I have been on my own since my early teens when my mother left. I later realized that was actually the best thing that could have happened for me.

After that, God continually led special people into my life, one after the other. Looking back, there was almost always someone there who truly cared about me, whether I deserved it or not, and each one had a hand in keeping me from falling away into no telling what kind of trouble. I am sad to say some will never know what they meant to me.

I am in a profession that I never would have guessed in a million years. Who ever grows up saying, "I want to be an Insurance Agent?" I think no one does. However, God had his own plan for me. An opportunity arose for me to work with Curtis Fuchs, a very successful insurance broker, who gave me more than a job and allowed me to share time with his family. This was very meaningful to me since I had no family of my own, and his was very special and dynamic.

Now I am greatly blessed with a wonderful wife, Nora, who is the kindest and most gentle woman I have ever known. Our daughters Candice, Donna, and Tabitha are beautiful young women and truly a joy in every way. I learned as much as I could from Curtis, and was determined not to waste that knowledge. I feel God gave me the tools and personality to build an agency that produces millions of dollars yearly, provides many jobs, and a place for thousands of agents to find quality products and people of integrity with which to work.

We were named one of "The Ten Most Dependable Agencies in The Eastern United States" by a major research firm, a great honor. Forbes Magazine published the formal announcement. There were thousands of agencies in the running for this prestigious acknowledgement. I work with some great people that deserve the credit for this distinction granted to our company. This is further proof that God brings people into our lives to help us fulfill the purpose he has for us. I could not have done this alone.

I am also blessed with musical ability that MUST be God given, as I was never able to take time for lessons. Yet, I have over twenty records that have made the charts, many into the top ten, I won Ed McMahon's "Next Big Star" contest and have played in a praise band for many years. I believe my sensitivity transferred to my music and allowed it to affect people in a positive way. To be honest, it still surprises me to see the success in that area. I suppose we hear ourselves differently than others hear us.

Without question, I could have been given a dramatically less challenging path to follow. However, would I treasure my family as much as I do if I had not grown up without one? In addition, would I appreciate the outdoors as much as I do had I not spent so much time locked away in a room? Would I care as much about the feelings and well-being of others? Would I have the empathy for people who are struggling? Would I be as genuinely appreciative of everything I have if I had not lived with nothing? Would I hold such value for genuine friendships if I had not been prevented from being with other children all of those years? How many children can say they actually *like* school? I LOVED to go to school. I suppose it was my escape from the dangers and stresses at home. Who can say if I would have had the favor that I have received from God if I had been dealt an easier life?

I was brought up hearing that I was worthless, unwanted, and that I would never amount to anything. Ultimately, those words became my strongest motivation. I simply had to prove those words false. I have a serious issue with people who use their past as an excuse to fail now and in the future. <u>We do have choices.</u> There was great wisdom in the script of the classic movie, "The Lion King," when Pumbaa said that we must "put our behind in the past."

For several moments, at a very young age, I thought I was going to die as my mother held the pistol to my temple. Now I cherish life even more because of the occurrence of things such as that. I think I must be here for a reason and I continue to strive to make the most of it to the best of my ability.

We are God's children. The Word tells us that it is His desire for us to have a healthy and prosperous life. Who are we to refuse that from Him?

I must say that I am convinced that the only explanation for my ability to endure the trials in my life is the belief and strength I receive from the following scriptures;

> *"When my mother and father forsake me, then the Lord will take me up."*
> *Psalm 27:10 KJV*

> *"A Father of the fatherless."*
> *Psalm 68:5a KJV*

> *"And we know that all things work together for good to them that love God, to them who are the called according to his purpose."*
> *Romans 8:28 KJV*

I truly do not know when or where I first heard these words, but I have known for quite some time and I have experienced God honoring these promises time and time again in my life.

While I still struggle daily to find peace within myself and to overcome the things ingrained in my mind as a child, I can honestly say that I love life and the adventure and beauty it offers. There is a wonderful world out there to explore. I was honored when asked to share my testimony for this important project, I must admit I did not feel qualified to do so, but I felt a connection to the people involved and wanted to be a part of this work. While this has been far from a complete accounting, I pray that it has meaning for those who read it.

Dr. Isaac Deas

 was born in New Haven, Connecticut. He is the Interfaith Chaplain of Hospice, Lake and Sumter County, Adjunct Professor for Lake/ Sumter Community College, Foundation Board member of Lake Sumter Community College, Guardian ad litem, Lake County and Board of Directors for the YMCA. Dr. Deas has a bachelors' degree in Social Work from the University of New Haven. He has three Masters' degrees: Public Administration, University of Connecticut, Counseling, University of New Haven, and Education from Columbia University. He has a Doctorate of Education from Columbia University.

Dr. Deas is the President and CEO of Deas Consulting and serves as Assistant Pastor at The Fathers Houses Christian Center, Leesburg, Florida.

Contact information: ideas2@comcast.net

I Am Still Rising

The Early Years

My name is Isaac Deas. I was born 15 April 1952 in New Haven, Connecticut. My mother still lives in my very first home, designed and built by my parents. They were married 56 years. New Haven is one of the oldest and most prosperous communities in the United States; its educational institutions reflect that age and richness. It was a wonderful place in which to grow up.

A prince, I felt that I should have been denied little. However, there was a fly in the ointment: my older sister. A flourishing sibling rivalry existed between us. She kept too close an eye on me, to my way of thinking. She told our parents everything, and seemed always to publicize when I was off the mark, but rarely when I got it right.

A typical boy, if there was a wrong place to be, that is where I usually was. Consequently, I received many spankings, not only from my parents, but also from the neighbors. Way back in the fifties, your neighbors cared enough to take part in your upbringing, and parents gratefully sanctioned their watchfulness. I could have done without their care and interest, of course. There were eyes everywhere. Where was justice in the world?

We were a cohesive family and we traveled a lot. Ours was an open house. There was no prejudice. We accepted people as they were. My mother owned a hair salon and later became a nurse. My father was a manager at nearby Yale University. He was a culinary graduate. Perhaps I love to cook and eat because he did! He was the strict one in the family. His messages were "Work Hard" and "Do Not Ask for Handouts." My mother was more lenient, loving and deeply caring always.

Naturally, Education with a capital E was encouraged. Both my parents always told us there is nothing that we cannot do. Education greased the wheels to get you there. "Education makes it possible." It was a family mantra. I obtained my B.A. in Social Work at Southern Connecticut State College. At the University of New Haven, I got my MA in Public Administration. At the University of Bridgeport, I got my M.A. in Counseling. I obtained both my M.A. and Doctorate in Education.

With my mother, sister and other kids in the neighborhood, I attended the Congregational Church.

When I grew older, I was drawn to the Baptist services.

Growing Up

I worked hard throughout elementary and high school; consequently, I was a high-achiever in academics as well as sports. Track was my main sport; how I loved to run! All work and no play makes for a dull fellow, I believed. Mine was a party life, but I passed with A's and B's. I had many friends and very good friends at that.

Drugs? Not me....

I began smoking pot in my freshman year of college. Prior to that, I was the clean athlete. My teammates elected me captain of the track team in my senior year; I was the first black captain in the school's history. Everyone I knew smoked pot—at least, those who were "cool" smoked pot.

Outside the ivy-covered walls of my rich environment what was happening? The Vietnam War, the MLK, Jr. march, Malcolm X, Black Panthers. However, it was all Rock-N-Roll and fast cars to my cool friends and me. We were above all that.

We experimented with hash and speed, but anything else was a "drug," and that meant hands-off.

One day in college, some scientist among us said, "Let's put coke in the pot and smoke it that way."

Because there were girls present and I was too cool to back out, I tried it. It was okay, but no big deal. The stakes were raised with the experimentation. This led to snorting cocaine once a week or at a concert. Then twice weekly, then three times, and so on it grew.

I was never a drinker. Perhaps I have been drunk twice in my whole life. Tequila, lemon, and salt was good, but while that was my first drunken episode, MD20-20, better known as "Mad-dog" wine, was my second and last one.

Married Life

I met my wife in church after I moved out of my parents' home to my own apartment. She was a soloist and very pretty with a nice body and very pleasing to the eye. I was immediately attracted to her. She had a three-year-old daughter from a previous marriage. Truly, she was my soul mate from the beginning. Her family was wider than mine was. She had 21 brothers and sisters by the same parents.

We had our home built to our own design. We were deeply in love with each other and life. Soon our son was born. We had it all.

I was the first black supervisor for the state of Connecticut's Juvenile Division. A probation officer for 3 years, I was a supervisor for 11 years. I was successful in my work and well respected. It was common knowledge that I was being groomed to take over the whole division. Everything was proceeding along the lines of the American Dream: I possessed a good job, a good wife, a good income, and good friends

Fall From Grace

Someone offered to introduce me to crack.

Who, me? No, that is a Drug... and a hands-off one at that.

I refused several times over a three-month period. However, curiosity and hunger for some new thrill, gnawed at my brain. Knowing I could never be hooked, and wanting to experiment further with drugs, I finally tried crack. Promptly, my system rejected it, and I threw up. I refuse to let anything get the best of me. I was determined to beat this bodily weakness, my body's natural rejection of this toxin. I continued experimenting, playing, until my system finally broke and hungrily grabbed onto the crack abuse. In no time at all, I was hooked. Practice makes perfect...

What was going on at this time? Everything was going well: I was supervisor of probation with an excellent salary. I was blessed with a beautiful wife who loved me dearly, and truly was my best friend. We had just built a new house from scratch, lived the good life in a good neighborhood, and we both drove new cars. We were well know and enjoyed the best relationships possible with family and friends. We had two beautiful children, a girl and a boy. As heavily involved in church and community work as I was in the Juvenile Division, I remained in denial for a long time until my life was affected in major ways by the addiction. First, I was late for work, then; I did not go to work. I lost weight, did not go home some nights. I lied to my wife, my family, and my good friends.

Therefore, I mastered crack without getting sick, but still I could not go out and buy it because I was Supervisor Deas. I was above going out to get it myself. I might be seen. I might be caught. I did not want anyone to know except those who got the drug for me. This went along until people started stealing the drug from me. In addition, I did not know how to cook it up to smoke myself. I depended on others who knew how to cook it, but not all the way. After I left, they would cook it more and smoke without me, my money buying their pleasure. Not fair. Why should I subsidize the thrill of others?

The only choice I had was to get the nerve to buy it myself.

That was my ultimate downfall.

It was scary at first but it got easier. I slipped out late at night to purchase my fix, but this left my wife wondering where I was and why I was out so late. "Another woman" sounded like a better reason to me than the truth of purchasing drugs.

I never confirmed or denied that another woman was in my life. I just let her mind wander in doubt and hurt. The deceit and cruelty of that action is the embodiment of the selfishness, the "I" of the druggie.

Crack is insidious. It grabs you before you know it. However, I was still Supervisor Deas in denial. I started missing work, coming in late, with no accountability. There were 14 juvenile offices. My office was always ranked one, two, or three in productivity. Cohesive, well run, mine was the model office. When my behavior changed, everyone knew there was something wrong but me. To me everything was status quo. Who knew I was doing this? No one except the few elect, I thought. Wrong. Denial was so deep that I believed the lie.

Drugs made me desperate. To raise funds for drugs, I sold my daughter's television, camera, and bike. I sold anything in the house I could get my hands on. My wife left me, but tried to put things in storage. We both visited the house in rotation, she to put things in storage, me, to plunder and sell stuff to get my needs filled. It was a race to see who could remove our worldly goods the fastest.

I went to treatment through the job for one month, and then got high two weeks after its completion. Our home went into foreclosure. My parents were both devastated. Both of them believed in Tough Love: "We love you but you can't come home doing drugs." Father, predictably, was more strict than Mother. While she was hurt, my father was hugely disappointed, and my sister was simply angry. The whole family ached with hurt, and disappointment. I literally had it all given to me on a silver platter, and blew it, just like the Prodigal Son.

I could not go to their home, so I lived on the streets. My mom, wife, and sister used contacts to put me in jail for sixteen weeks, hoping I would lose the need for drugs while there. I got high the very day I was released. Why? I met and made friends with the drug pushers in jail. Therefore, upon release they told me where to go to get the best drugs. With the mention of their names, I was set. Crazy thinking. A roller coaster ride of drugs...

Back to the streets I went. I existed in NYC and Connecticut crack houses, or slept in cars, on park benches, in storefronts, cardboard boxes, or any other home I could find. I lied, conned, and cheated, but I was never violent or a thief. Because I had the gift of gab, I could and did talk others into doing what I wanted. Women supplied my primary needs of food, shelter, sex, and drugs. Crazy life: I was panhandling, running schemes, conning people. I knew the street life well and I was good at it. You can always make money if you think through the process. Education makes it all possible. After all, practice makes perfect.

Overdosing was a regular happening: using too much or getting bad drugs mixed with who knew what. The result was stomach cramps, followed by endless dry heaves, and then sleeping for a full day without waking up. Why? Because you are up all day and night, running your scheme. Shakes, nose running, joints hurting, you get cold then hot then cold again, then hot again, your body searching for sanity—or sanctuary from itself.

The only way to come down from being so high is to take a downer. For me, the hands-down favorite was heroin, another drug that I swore that I would never use. Repulsed by needles, I snorted it. This also makes you throw up, but the reward afterwards is a beautiful high. Alternatively, so we tell ourselves…

Things I saw while in the life: Women selling their daughters to pushers for drugs. People dead with needles still in their arms. Other junkies pulling out the needles and sticking them in their own arms. Men prostituting themselves, women, the same, me, the same. People, both men and women, beaten up for non-payment. Police selling drugs or keeping them for themselves. People being shot or stabbed. The mole people living underground. Yes, here in America.

Sometimes I felt hunger, but had no money for food. Restaurant trashcans beckoned. Outside the restaurants where the waiters knew me, I patiently waited for them to discard their unused food. Why not? They would only throw it out anyway. Occasionally, Mom would feed me if I could visit her without Dad being there. Sometimes friends provided a meal.

Nevertheless, the cafes and restaurants were always dependable. My dear long-suffering wife finally began divorce proceedings. By then I was so far removed from reality, I knew nothing about it—or remembered nothing. Later, while in rehabilitation down South, someone told me I was now divorced. I felt immense sadness about letting down my beloved soul mate and friend.

One day I went to get high and God had taken the taste away. In my prayers, I asked Him to take the taste away. Two years into my addiction, He did. I called Mom and she said she had been waiting for my call. Once again God had revealed to Mom in a dream what He was about to do. Three days later, it happened. God always kept her informed about what He was going to do with me. Did she worry? Yes. Did she cry? Yes. Did God come through as He said He would? Yes. Did she ever doubt God? What do you think?

Truly, I was the Prodigal Son. My Mom prayed me through. She never gave up hope and never gave up on me. She kept that telephone line to God hot and humming on my behalf. I was not 40 years old.

Dawning of a New Day/
Breaking the Spirit of Addiction

On the advice of a friend, I journeyed to Florida for rehabilitation.

"Youth Challenge" was a long-term substance abuse rehabilitation center for men aged 18 and above in Wildwood, in Central Florida. I was twenty-two months in treatment—although God had already freed me. I did well at Youth Challenge and eventually became a staff member. As such, I soon began pouring into the lives of others in the program and in the community.

The first thing I saw on my arrival was Confederate flags and trucks with shotguns in the back. This was my first trip to the South. I was shocked and not a little afraid. We had no relatives living in the South, but I had heard the stories. Was this really 1991?

Two white men pulled up, asked if I was Isaac. When I nodded, they told me to get in the truck between them. Fresh off the streets, I said "No, thanks. I'll ride in the cab in the back." I did not know where I was, or where I was going, but I watched for landmarks, just in case I had to make a break. I had no money to go back home, but I was not going to be killed willingly.

One of the most shocking facts of life in Florida in the 1990s was the blatant prejudice, still hanging around like a miasma from the swamps. With all that was going on in the world, this place was still pulling the race card.

As we pulled up to Youth Challenge, I saw other men working and walking around. Most of them looked as underfed as I was. My weight was 98 pounds at that time. Normally, I was a hefty 187 pounds. I was "half the man" I had been, literally. And, so it seemed, were my new colleagues.

Not a very modern set-up, still Youth Challenge seemed paradise to me, after living the hell of the streets of NYC. I remember feeling cold in Central Florida's November 1991. This 98-pound skeleton did not have very many clothes, and certainly no fat to keep me warm, but I made do.

The routine for clients here included washing and ironing our own clothes, keeping our rooms straight, tidy, and clean, and daily work both inside and outside. We were kept busy and occupied—and challenged. I immediately received the task of raking leaves, and I hated every moment of that menial work. Outside jobs included cutting grass in the rain and the scorching heat of the sun, raking leaves, pulling weeds, and in general, "tidying the garden." No matter what you did outside you always felt too hot or too cold. Of course, I wanted to help, but I wanted it on my terms. Just let me sleep (inside!) and do what I want to do and things would be great.

Wrong. Very quickly, I learned I was IN the band, and not leading it this time...

My first inside job assignment was cleaning the bathrooms. I was outraged. After all, I had three Master's degrees and was half-way through my Doctorate. The nerve of these people—giving ME that job! Did they not know who I was?

The smelly bathroom job was mine for five months. In that time, I became the best bathroom cleaner that I could be. When I cleaned it, everyone knew—it did not smell anymore. I began to take pride in my low-level job.

After that special challenge, I graduated to the kitchen with its preparing and serving of meals. This was much more acceptable, and I was soothed to my soul. I ate all I wanted. Now this was Power: people had to wait for me to serve. Cool. This is how it should be, but—the challenges continued. After meals, I still had to work outside. Bummer.

I saw many discouraged men. Some left the program and came back later. Some were rebellious and complained about everything. I just kept my complaints to myself, mumbling to God like a small boy, and silently observed the activity of the clients and staff of Youth Challenge. Because I was never caught up in anything, like game playing and web weaving, many people gravitated my way. I was educated; I helped them write letters, helped with their schoolwork. I counseled them when I needed counseling myself.

God was beginning his work in me.

"Promoter" was my final job at Youth Challenge, though I did not know it at the time. Standing outside stores all over Florida from Thursdays through Saturdays, I sold key-chains and tee shirts. With the gift of the gab, I was good at this. Promoters kept 10% of our gross. I became so good and made so much, that I was promoted to Head of Promotions. This meant I received 10% of everyone's gross! Cash is a great motivator.

We attended church three times per week. One grey, overcast day at early morning chapel, I was praying in a corner. God urged me to think about the people I had hurt or disappointed. As I thought of them, I began to weep.

The sun came out of the cloud for a brief moment and I could feel what I thought was the heat of the sun covering my body through the windows at the top of the room. I looked around. The sun only hit that one spot where I was praying. I could feel its heat, and I could feel the Son's hand on me. Something starting above my head descended over the whole of my body. The sensation was almost that I was wetting myself. I tingled to my toes—I felt great.

Then His Life Secret hit me powerfully: the True "Trip" is freedom through forgiveness. Wow.

God revealed to my mother three days prior what He was going to do "in three days." When I finally left the chapel for my room, the mail arrived. There was a letter from my mother. In it, she told me exactly what "would happen."

In fact, it just had.

LifeStreams: A New Beginning

After twenty-two months, in 1993 God opened a door for me at LifeStreams, an agency for Mental Health Counseling in Lake and Sumter Counties in Florida.

A friend of mine at Youth Challenge who worked his way up to went to LifeStreams first. He started working at the substance abuse division, naturally. When he heard that I had also "graduated" from YC, he invited me to come in for an oral interview. As I had recently promoted key-chains and tee shirts around Orlando with no little success and with God in the driver's seat, I was confident in my skill level to promote myself.

I was offered the job the very day I interviewed, and was employed by LifeStreams as a counselor for seven years. The following week I began as a substance abuse counselor and worked the position for nearly a year. Beginning with 10, my caseload grew to almost 100 as the people came and went.

Because I could feel their pain, most of the clients related to me. I did not judge or disrespect them. We worked with males and females. I kept things basic and down-to-earth, but my long-range desire was to work with youth. They were my primary focus.

After a year, my supervisor allowed me to begin working with younger clients. I started with six and it grew very quickly. Soon, the Board of Education (BOE) was sending me people. As a result, other agencies began to hear about me and sent clients to work with me. There were job offers from a few, but I remained loyal to LifeStreams and its established youth program, Treatment Abuse Substance Counseling (TASC). Soon I took over that program—and began my own counseling service, Deas Consulting.

I am a self-starter. Taking the initiative is something I have done all my life. I fear no risk-taking. Many of my decisions are based on instinct, a "feeling" about the outcome of some action or someone. I am seldom wrong. Some of my colleagues really did not know how to take me, as I am not in their mold. Yes, I am definitely a team player, but if you will not play— why, I will go it alone. I never spoke of my educational background. They assumed simply that I was a drug-using "nig from the streets," now clean and trying to be productive. They never guessed those years before in my Connecticut job, I had not only run an office very successfully, but also trained others to do the same.

When I went to meetings, it was assumed that I was merely the guy from LifeStreams who liked to work with troubled youth. I liked it that way and remained quiet and humble—unless pushed too far by a graceless individual. Then I would switch to assertive mode, and communicate!

My adult clients at LifeStreams were free of racial bias. Even the "good ole boy" clients respected me because of my stance: I was as non-threatening as I was non-judgmental. My mien was peaceful. How could I do my work otherwise?

They heard my message: I feel your pain, baby. I have been there. I am you and you are I.

On group days, I took the youth to Eustis Park. Merchants would often comment that I was the Pied Piper with my following queue of 16 youth. I loved these outings, loved being with them, and the "badder" they were, the better I loved them. The more dysfunctional the being, the greater the challenge, and I love a challenge. The program I started gained much notoriety and is still functioning today. Most clients today, however, come to my current practice in Tavares.

The year 2002 was a very special and blessed year for me. I began Deas Consulting as CEO and President. I became an inter-faith chaplain for Hospice of Lake and Sumter Counties (HLS). I was asked to be an Adjunct Professor at Lake Sumter Community College.

The Father's House

In 2003, The Father's House became reality.

I was a "People Person." He was a Teacher.

When I told him I was a former drug addict from New York City, I think the pastor was a bit apprehensive. The color difference was not a problem, but as he was raised in lily-white Kentucky where few People of Color lived, diversity in our cultures was of some concern. A good fit, black and white, we complemented one another. Our bond has been proven since in fire, and is as strong as steel. We work well together, albeit with occasional disagreements. He is a great teacher with an open mind and heart.

The pastor and his wife, another couple, and I met, sharing ideas about a new kind of church called The Father's House, not a dozen years ago. We numbered 20 at our first service. Today we have a new church building to accommodate our 700 members, increasing with every service.

Community work is my strength and magnet. Many of our members joined the church because they heard or saw me somewhere. God has given me a gift to attract others. People are people, the color line or economics make no difference to me.

Four years after our beginning, I was ordained. The first Youth pastor, the first Singles' pastor, I also supervise the Jail and Hospital Ministry. I love preaching, teaching, encouraging and visiting the forgotten in our jails and hospitals.

Most of the counseling at the church is conducted by me. I advise the pastor and the staff when required. The pastor has blessed and encouraged me in my gifts as a community person. My heart and natural bent is for the hurting, lonely, discouraged, and dysfunctional. The pastor likes to dream and sets the vision and tone for The Father's House. We both minister to the flock with our individual gifts.

In 2003, I was ordained as a Minister in The Father's House.

Every day I thank my God, my Father, for "raking those leaves" in my life and teaching me how to do it for myself—and how to teach others to do it for themselves.

Still Rising

A member of numerous community boards, I have won many awards for community service.

I maintain various successful and satisfying contracts with community agencies. I am blessed and proud because:

God saw fit to save me and use me for His service, my father saw me sober, and functioning before he died, my mother visits my house and witnesses the result of her prayers.

In order to leave an impact legacy practice the following:

- ✛ Remember your message is your life,
- ✛ develop and maintain a healthy family because in the end they are all you'll have,
- ✛ never underestimate the importance of education,
- ✛ keeping faith in your ability to overcome obstacles that are placed in your path,
- ✛ never turn back,
- ✛ love yourself,
- ✛ learn to work harder on yourself than your job,
- ✛ help others grow when you can, and
- ✛ get involved in your community.

Michael Fuchs

lives in North Carolina with his wife Kirsten, his son Brandt, and daughters Haley and Brielle. Michael is the owner of DataBridge, a consulting company specializing in Microsoft SharePoint development and training (www.GetSharePoint.com).

He is the founder of Collide with Christ (www.CollideWithChrist.org), a ministry to men that focuses on uniting men to live, fight, and finish well. CWC leads retreats and conferences for men with a concentration on developing intimate friendships and emphasizing the necessity of small groups.

Contact information: Michael@collidewithchrist.com

God Likes Me!

Living a Lie

It's Friday, 3:30 AM on a brisk November morning in 2000 as I turn off the alarm and roll out of bed. A quick shower, a cup of coffee and off to work. I am always the first to arrive, usually by 4:30 am. It is a typical office; we import embroidery and apply it to shirts, hats, towels and the like. We started the business about a year and a half ago, just two of us working out of my basement. Today we have 15 employees and we are continuing to grow. Our hours are 8 am to 5 pm, but I come in early because by the time our staff comes in at 8:00 am there is not a lot of down time to get to the work on my desk.

I work a lot these days... 90 to 100 hours a week, but it is a new business and as anyone starting a new business knows, you have to put in a few years of hard work to be successful. I do not see my wife and three children much these days because I am working so much but that is just one of the sacrifices you have to make to be successful. I am doing it for them after all; paying the bills, saving for a new house and money for the kid's college education.

Everything is good these days, surely a lot better than most of my past: battles with Attention Deficit Disorder (ADD) and depression and my inconsistent employment (That is a nice way to say I had a tough time holding down a job.).

Saturday night we had a company Christmas party and as I was addressing the employees, thanking everyone for their dedication and hard work, I made a comment about this company being God's business. I do not know exactly what I said... it probably sounded real good, but it was only words. Do not get me wrong, I grew up in church and considered myself a Christian but I had not been to church since I left my childhood home and certainly did not have a personal relationship with God.

Sunday morning I am at work, as usual, and I get a call from my wife Kirsten. She tells me that my brother Brian is coming by to pick up the kids and take them to church with him (for the second week in a row) and that she is going with them today. As soon as I heard that, something in me began to scream, "You can't let your brother take your family to church!" I told Kirsten I was on my way home and that I would take them myself.

The service was surprisingly okay and I actually took notes. One of the points the Pastor spoke about that week was to Love Someone Enough to Tell Them the Truth. This really spoke to me because I had needed to talk to my partner for a long time about his performance and, I was sure, this was the nudge I needed. Little did I know that I was the one who was about to be told the truth.

Monday morning my assistant, who I had just hired a month before, asked to see me. She sat down and asked me about my comment at the Christmas party regarding this being God's business. She proceeds to tell me that she does not see any evidence of God in this business at all. She tells me that I am an arrogant man and very selfish with my time. In her opinion, my priorities were very out of whack. There were three marriages on the verge of divorce (one of them mine). My wife and I had just decided to get divorced and had planned on waiting until after the holidays to tell the kids. She went on to say that, there is no joy in this business; just a lot of striving and it is a very stressful place to work. Then she suggested that we have a prayer meeting each morning. Why I did not fire her right there, I will never know. I have no idea why I even considered her suggestion. I had never read the Bible, nor been to a prayer meeting but for some reason I said yes and the next day six of us started to meet at 7:00 am.

The Truth

The truth is she was right. What was worse is that she had only hit the tip of the iceberg. I was an arrogant man, extremely selfish with my time and my priorities were out of whack. My going to work at 4:30 in the morning under the guise of doing whatever it took to make this business successful was a farce. I would arrive early in the morning not to get a jump on work; however, to view pornography on the Internet. In years prior, I had viewed pornographic magazines and movies, but for the last four years, I had a three-hour a day addiction. It was a bondage that was ruling my life, taking me into work on weekends, and farther away from my family. Compared to so many other habits or addictions, it seemed harmless to me. It was free. No one could look in your eyes or smell your breath and tell that you had been looking at it and it was not hurting anyone, right? Boy was I wrong!

My work had become a great escape because it is the place where people who were telling me I was doing a great job surrounded me. It was a place where I was getting a pat on the back, a place where I was making progress, solving problems, and being challenged. A place where people listened to me and actually cared what I was saying and thinking. It was the place where I received validation. This business was, in no uncertain terms, my "salvation." Things were finally going my way. I was finally going to be able to prove to everyone that I was not a failure. That I had what it takes.

In actuality, I was mismanaging the business terribly. The only thing I was concerned about was growing the business as fast as possible: the bigger, the faster, the better! Anyone's suggestion of slowing down and planning for growth was met with great resistance from me… I would shut them down with belittling comments telling them they had no vision. That they had no confidence or courage and, if all else failed, I would remind them whom it was that got the company to where it was. The truth was we needed help in the area of planning and budgeting but I did not want to appear weak by saying so. Reality was that I was in bondage to pornography, spending 3 hours a day on the internet. I was working 7 days a week, over 90 hours a week, to escape the pain of a broken marriage. Once again, I had put Kirsten at the bottom of my list of priorities. My wife and I had become roommates… passing in the hall as I would come and go from work.

Work was an escape to avoid my children that I did not know how to communicate with anymore. I did so under the pose of, "this is what it takes to get ahead," "you have to put in a few years of hard work to be successful," "I'm doing this for my family and to put the kids through college." In truth, it had nothing to do with my family or being successful. It was simply a place of refuge. It was an acceptable place, by society standards, to retreat. For me, it was also a place where I would, hopefully… finally, get my dad's approval. You see, I still had this void inside of me, this longing for approval, which I was medicating with pornography and by keeping very, very busy.

In this little prayer meeting, and I must admit calling it that is a little deceiving, we opened and closed the meeting with prayer, but for the most part we just talked and began to discuss what was going on in our lives. In this meeting I agreed to step down from my throne and let God be in charge. Today, I can say I was not really sure what that meant, other than I remember it being a place where I didn't have to lead or have all the answers… a place where I could relax and even ask

Multiple Streams of Success

questions. Moreover, to be honest, as I began to feel safe enough in the group, God began to change me. Still today, I am confident that the prayer God rushed to answer was this, "God, do whatever it takes to change me!"

A New Beginning

People coming together in a small group, being open and honest and asking for God's help is a very powerful thing. It is the reason I am so fond of small groups. I have witnessed God change so many lives in this setting. In that group, I received a heart transplant.

> *A new heart also will I give you, and a new spirit will I put within you: and I will take away the stony heart out of your flesh, and I will give you an heart of flesh.*
> *Ezekiel 36:26 KJV*

God had given me a new heart and with it His approval. Somehow, in the midst of my arrogance, selfishness, and ugliness He loved me: no, more than that… God liked me and was proud of me… the approval that I had so long been seeking from my father… I now had from the Creator of the universe. Moreover, with it, this striving, hard charging guy was put at ease. God removed the pornography addiction within a moment. I went home that day and was watching TV when a

Victoria's Secret commercial came on and I had to leave the room because I was repulsed. God used the very thing that had kept me in bondage to turn my stomach. He is so cool! I asked for and received my prayer language in that small group. I had degenerative disks C5-C6 in my neck that caused me to go to the chiropractor twice a week. My brother laid hands on me and prayed for me and God instantly healed my neck.

The morning of January 8, 2001, we had been meeting for about 5 weeks. I am in the small group and I tell everyone that Kirsten and I are telling the kids we are getting a divorce that night and I threw out the question, "Why don't I feel bad about getting a divorce?" I actually felt at peace about the situation. Yet I had begun to read God's word and it was very clear what He thought. I went on to say, "We tried and it just didn't work." Then my business partner said, "Tried? When could you have possibly tried? You are always at work!" Those words hit me like a stake going through my heart. Then my general manager went on to tell us what it feels like to be a 9-year-old girl when your dad leaves (my middle daughter was nine at the time) and I was filleted. As I sat there crying, love and "like" for my wife sprang forth from my heart. I raced home to plead with her to reconsider our decision and worse case, to ask her that we not tell the children that night. When I had finished telling her what had happened to me that morning, without any "if only's" or "you have to's" Kirsten said, "I never wanted a divorce anyway." Just like that... God had changed both our hearts.

With all that God had begun to do in and through me, there were still consequences from poor decisions I had made and the person I had become. As of the printing of this book, in early 2008, I have just completed paying off a large tax debt from that business going under.

In 2004, I had a son who headed off to college that would barely speak to me because of my absenteeism as a father for so many years. This past year God has restored our relationship and we are now working together in a new successful business.

In 2005, Kirsten and I spent 11 months and 14 days separated in large part due to the fact that I had not made her the priority in my life that God intended. Today we are best friends who enjoy each other's company. We are a team living each day together with anticipation of what God is going to do next.

For 10 years, I took medication for Attention Deficit Disorder and in 2004, God healed me of ADD. The truth is I have too many stories of His rescues, favor, healing, and His incredible love for me than I have room here to write.

In preparing this chapter for a book subtitled real life stories about faith, hope, success, and overcoming adversity, I often felt compelled to have three steps to follow or four points for you to apply. I am a big believer in practical application and, at the same time, I cannot tell you how many books I have read that were supposed to help make me more productive or efficient by following several steps and yet somehow those never seemed to work very well for me. I think men, especially, need to know what they are supposed to do. "Tell me what I'm supposed to do to fix it and let me at it."

So, with that said, there is one thing I want to assure you of and one thing I want to encourage you to do.

I want to assure you that God likes you!

That is right, I said "likes" you. Do you believe it? For most of us, we do not like ourselves very much and for that reason, we find it very difficult to believe

God could. Most of us walk around with the knowledge that God loves us, but we perceive it as more of an obligatory thing. God is love… He has to love us, right? Let me say it again, God likes you! He more than loves you as a parent loves a child. He likes hanging out with you. He sent His only Son to die for your sins as an expression of His great love for you, but He also enjoys your laugh and your odd sense of humor. He is crazy about you!

Say, it aloud right now, "God likes me!" Say it again, "GOD LIKES ME!" Before you said anything, before you did anything, before you were a thing, God liked you and He still does. Is He proud of everything you have done or are doing? No. However, He does like you and who He created you to be!

I am reminded of a friend of mine who got a little busy, like we all do from time to time, and he realized one day how his quiet time with God had been pushed out of his schedule. He decided to set time aside each day to spend with God, time to be quiet and listen. After four weeks, he began to get frustrated that he had not heard from God and he asked, "God, I am listening. Why won't you speak to me?" and God said, "I didn't realize I needed to. I just like spending time with you."

God was telling him, "I like you and I enjoy your company."

> *And Jesus, when he was baptized, went up*
> *straightway out of the water: and, lo,*
> *the heavens were opened unto him,*
> *and he saw the Spirit of God descending like a*
> *dove, and lighting upon him:*
> *And lo a voice from heaven, saying,*
> *This is my beloved Son,*
> *in whom I am well pleased.*
> *Matthew 3:16-17 KJV*

Before Jesus did anything, God wanted Jesus to know He was proud of Him and He wants you to know the same thing.

If this is a little hard to believe or maybe you are thinking it is even a little silly, try this. Ask Him. "God, do you really like me?" Close this book, be quiet for a few minutes, and ask Him.

What would He say? I told you! Moreover, because He likes you, lighten up a little bit, give yourself a little breathing room and begin to like yourself. Forget what your parents say or have said, forget what others say or have said. Somehow, along the way, most of us begin to pose for the world around us. Becoming more of whom we believe they will like rather than being our true selves.

I am sure that as you read this there is a thing or two that you know you should start or stop doing. As you have heard part of my story, I am sure there is a "hidden" thing or two in your life that you would be glad to be rid of. What is restricting your level of life and joy today? Is it a troubled relationship with your spouse or child, depression, an addiction to drugs, alcohol, pornography, or something else? What is it that you are using to "medicate" the pain or loneliness? What do you do when you get stressed and need to blow off a little steam? Am I getting a little too personal? Here is why I ask… As long as you keep a "thing" hidden, it cannot be healed. Jesus often asked, "Do you want to be healed?" Kind of a curious question isn't it?

One of the most straightforward verses in the entire Bible to me is

And the people, when they knew it, followed him: and he received them, and spake unto them of the kingdom of God, and healed them that had need of healing.
Luke 9:11 KJV

And healed those who needed healing… I often wonder how many in the crowd that day were too proud, too embarrassed, or too ashamed to come forward and admit they needed healing.

How about you?

Do you need healing?

It still exists today just as it did then.

Do you believe?

My encouragement to you is this; Ask God for help and give him permission to do whatever it takes to help. There are no three-step formulas here. Just make your requests known to God and give Him permission to work in that area of your life. In addition, find someone you trust. A friend, a family member, your pastor, a small group and let them know about your decision and what you have asked God to do. Enlist their help to stand with you and watch God work.

If there is one thing I understand less and less as I do it, it is prayer. Moreover, I can tell you it is revolutionary and it works. From my own experience, I can tell you there appears to be one kind of prayer that God rushes to answer. The prayer begins with "Change me Lord..." In addition, for a reason I do not understand, that prayer brought to light in the midst of other people seems to get immediate attention. I have given this a lot of thought and here is what I have deduced... Again, this is just my opinion, but it seems, if I trust others enough to be real, open, and honest, somehow it is a sign of faith that I trust God, too.

Tell someone today that God likes him or her and *know* that He likes you, too!

Ken Scrubbs

is a native of Louisiana. He was born in New Orleans where he attended public schools in the State of Louisiana. He is a graduate from the historical Black College Grambling University in Grambling, LA.

While attending Grambling State University he earned a double major: B.S. degree in Accounting and Data Processing in 1975. He was also a member of the Grambling State's football team under the nationally acclaimed football Coach Eddie Robinson.

For 20 years, Ken worked in corporate America. In 1991, harkening to the call of God on His life became an ordained as a minister of the gospel. Ken received His Bachelor of Arts in Theology from Crosland Christian University.

He has been married to Linda for 34 years after meeting her in college. The Scrubbs' have three wonderful children: Cymonda, April and James. His daughters are graduates of the University of Florida, Gainesville. In addition, James is a graduate of Lander University in Greenwood, SC.

Ken is currently the Community Outreach Pastor of the Christian Care Center a division of First Baptist Church of Leesburg, in Leesburg, Florida. He has invested innumerable hours and works tirelessly to provide directions for the community that he serves. Ken is committed to helping children's dreams become a reality and being a positive impact in their lives. He is responsible for the following youth centered ministries: Campus Ministry Coordinator, Director of The Micah Project (Mentoring Children), and After School tutoring

110

Program, the Neighborhood Accountability Board, and Peer Mediation Program through the Department of Juvenile Justice. Ken is also the Director of a Prison Ministry in the Largest Federal Prison in America; the Federal Correctional Complex at Coleman; in Coleman Florida.

He has received the following awards and acknowledgments: Governor's Mentor of the Year. (Best Practice Model) in the state of Florida, Panelist at Successful Partnerships Workshops for the White House Office of Faith-Based and Community Initiative Conference, lead discussion on Florida's At-Risk Youth, Member of the State Steering Committed for the Department of Juvenile Justice Appointed by Governor Jeb Bush to the State of Florida Faith Based Advisory Board, Member of the Department of Education Faith and Community Advisory Board, Appointed to Florida Disaster Relief Board by Gov Charlie Christ 2007, Runner-up in the Department of Education Community Leader of the Year in the State of Florida 2006, Selected by Florida Monthly Magazine as one of Twenty-Two most Intriguing Floridians Who Excels in Service to Others 2006, appointed as Chairman for the State of Florida Drop-Out Prevention Task Force, by Commissioner John Wynn 2007, and Member of the African American Black Republican Advisory Council .

Contact information: kenscrubbs@fbcleesburg.org

Some Say Money Doesn't Fall From the Sky—I Beg to Differ!

Years ago, I heard a sermon on tangible faith. The Word says

> *"Now faith is the*
> *substance of things hoped for,*
> *the evidence of things not seen."*
> *Hebrews 11:1 KJV.*

Therefore, could something we hope for be tangible at the same time? I have learned that the Lord engages us where we are in life, He establishes the path of transformation, and He can and will do the seemingly impossible to get our attention. We have heard stories from our elders and others about how God has worked in their lives – stories about how God is an 'on-time God.' Little did I know how 'on-time' He could and would be. Following is a story about the beginning of my walk with the Lord in which I became accountable to Him. Before this, all of my life I held him accountable to my requests (prayers), as we so often do. Yet we live our lives free of a true commitment to His perfect will for us. Never really accepting that we were created for His Glory...

If two doors stood before you, one marked "Miracles" and one-marked "Blessings," which one would you choose? I believe God has something planned for our life that is more than a miracle: a life filled with His blessings. Of course, a blessing is not nearly as impressive and exciting as a miracle, yet both are supernatural and both come from God. I am convinced that God's best for us is to live in His blessings, not only to expect His miracles.

The year of 1992 was a year of great transition for the Scrubb's family; many things in our life were changing. After twenty years in corporate America I seemingly had accomplished and accumulated a good life for me and my family—a beautiful, suburban house with a pool, cars, $400 Brooks Brothers suits, $250 Italian shoes, $50 Burberry shirts, $45 ties, as well as power lunches and powerful friends. It seemed to be the life that most poor little boys, as I had been, never experienced. I was living the American Dream, with little regard for God. We had been provided for but I was the one taking the credit and not giving it the ultimate provider—God. Spiritually I was in the desert—it was to become clear that my life of running from the call of God was done, and the time had come for me to be accountable to HIM.

God gave a miracle to the children of Israel that lasted the entire 40 years they were in the desert. Each morning, manna fell supernaturally from heaven. All the people had to do was to go out and gather it up. But this was not God's best. He wanted to move his people out of the desert and into the Promised Land, to move them past the need for daily miracles and into a life of blessings.

In this longest-running miracle in history, we can see different ways in which blessings are better than miracles. The Israelites were in a crisis. There was no food or water in the desert, so without a daily miracle, they would have died. In contrast, the Promised Land was rich and well watered. There, the Israelites were blessed with an abundance of everything. When the crisis was over, the daily miracles stopped. So let me ask you, which is better, manna every morning—or an abundant variety of things to eat? <u>Miracles come in a crisis, but blessings keep the crisis from coming.</u>

After living my life very selfishly for years, focused on what I wanted to do, making countless bad decisions concerning my life, and taking for granted the tremendous opportunities I had been afforded by God to make a impact in the kingdom for His glory, I was now face to face with life's reality. I was getting older and my body was showing signs of my wreckless disregard for it during my younger years playing football. I had to vacate my job in the fast lane—I was experiencing increasing numbness on the left side of my body—and I was going to have to have surgery on my spinal cord. This was the result of injuries that I incurred playing football in college as a wide receiver.

It would take two of these surgeries to "heal" by body—it would take the mercy and grace of God to "heal" my soul. After surgery, I was bed bound for a long period. I had much time to think. After the second surgery I was done, spent, at the end of my rope. The healing process was long and painful. I did not know what to do—and was able to do very little. However, after the second surgery, though I was instructed not to move out of bed, I slid out of the bed, gave up, and gave my life to Him entirely. I prayed to God – that my life was His to do as He willed – and I understood that if I was going to make it I would need Him and now I knew that! For the next three years I spent hours praying, journaling, and studying the Bible.

After the two surgeries and not able to return to work, we were living on long-term disability pay so we did not have a lot of money and bills were mounting. Our two daughters were in college. I was no longer the provider and leader in our family. Now there was a new leader. It was Jesus Christ and we all would have to learn to wait and trust Him and seek His will—and above all be obedient to Him.

> *Beloved, think it not strange concerning the*
> *fiery trial which is to try you, as though some*
> *strange thing happened unto you:*
> *But rejoice, inasmuch as ye are*
> *partakers of Christ's sufferings;*
> *that, when his glory shall be revealed,*
> *ye may be glad also with exceeding joy.*
> *1 Peter 4:12-13 KJV*

Miracles provide just enough to get you through. God instructed His people to pick up just enough manna for their family's immediate needs. Those who gathered more and tried to hoard it found it bred worms. In contrast, blessings come in abundance. God's purpose is to bless you so much, that you can start giving to others. In fact, God wants you to prosper so much that your blessings can become someone else's miracles. Miracles come in small amounts but blessings come in great abundance.

There was a point when I was able to leave the house and start participating in life. I could not work sitting at a desk putting pressure on the surgical repaired part of my body (my neck)—the recovery from my surgery would not allow me to sit for any period. I was, however able to participate in coaching my son's baseball team. Our son, James, was 13 and considered a top 100-baseball player in the State of Florida and playing AAU baseball. On this particular Saturday, we were at Dr Phillips High School, Orlando, and things were going well for the team, but, personally, I was not sure where to turn. My wife and I arrived at the ballpark with less than a quarter of a tank of gas and five dollars to our name. I cannot began to tell you how depleted I felt, knowing that whatever the outcome of the game; I would be faced with the reality that we were completely out of money. I had no idea where the next penny would come from. Our family income had dropped significantly. I was now on long-term disability, which was a long way from a senior financial analyst at a Fortune 500 Company.

To our way of thinking, receiving a miracle marks one as a person of great faith, but that is not necessarily true. God did not miraculously feed the

Israelites because of their great faith, confessions or glorious praise and worship. That whole generation was so filled with doubt and unbelief that they could not enter into the Promised Land, yet God still provided a miracle for them every single day!

Although we did win the game, Linda informed me that she could not find the last five dollars—so just when you think things cannot get any worse—they do. We were faced with the fact that we may not have enough gas to get home and no food in the house. As we departed the stadium, I felt very small. I had lived a rather humble life as a child—not a lot of anything, food included—and now here I was in that place again, this time with my family. In spite of this, I had to believe that God knew and He was at the helm ready to display His power and provisions for His glory.

Ultimately, God wants to bless the works of our hands. In the desert, the Israelites watched God work for them, but once they reached the Promised Land, the manna ceased. God said, "Now I want you to sow. Whatever you sow, I will bless, and you will reap a hundredfold." When we put our hands to work, God will work with us and bless us exceedingly abundantly above all we can ask or think. We receive His favor. Although

God's blessings may take the form of things, blessings begin as His divine favor. Everywhere we go, this favor hovers over us and caused things to work out for our good. In a miracle, God works for you; in a blessing God works with you.

As we were leaving Dr Phillips—it did not take long for Linda to go to sleep, I am sure the depression had something to do with it. As I departed the parking lot and merged on to the freeway, I wondered what were we going to do. Would I humble myself and ask friends for money, call home and ask for support, or go to the pawnshop and pawn more jewelry? It was clear that I would have to do something I would prefer not to do, and whatever that was; it would leave me feeling less of a man I than I professed to be. As I peered out onto the long road home, know that when I got there it would present some tough decisions I genteelly whispered a prayer to the Lord— "I ask Him was He going to take care of us, as His word promised?"

This may surprise you, but miracles are mainly reserved for sinners and new believers who are just beginning to experience the things of God. Miracles are like a jump-start to get us into a life of blessings. But God does not want us to operate on jump-starts every single day. This does not mean that mature believers will never face a crisis and need a miracle. There will never come a time when we do not need miracles anymore.

However, as we walk in God's blessings, we find that we do not need them daily and our crises are further and further apart. By definition, a miracle is a divine intervention into the laws of nature. Manna falling from heaven, huge flocks of quail appearing in the desert, the Red Sea parting—these are all examples of God using His power to momentarily override the natural systems He has put in place. In contrast, blessings work hand in hand with the natural laws. Miracles work against natural laws, but blessings cooperate with nature.

After I whispered my prayer, I refocused my attention on the highway, and at that moment, as I looked into the distance I saw what appeared to be pieces of paper floating in the air. There was, however, something different about these pieces of paper - they seemed to be cut into perfect rectangles; yes like money! I thought to myself this could not be. I figured it was my imagination playing tricks on me in my desperate state, and of course, the enemy of our soul (Satan) had his say as well. He said things like "do not be foolish, money does not fall out of the sky." However, as I got closer it seemed that, that is exactly what was happening. I pulled over to see what was happening—I gently opened the door. I wanted to be inconspicuous, as I surely did not want to wake Linda up and her ask me what was I doing. And, if it wasn't money after all, then I would look like the very thing the enemy said seconds ago, a fool.

I eased the door open and looked under the car pretending as if there was a problem with the tires. Then I got out and noticed that there was a new five-dollar bill lying in front of the car. I could not believe what my eyes were seeing; money was lying all around the car. As I walked around car, I began picking up money all around the car, five dollars here and ten dollars there. Across the Interstate, I saw what I believed to be more money floating toward the ground. I looked to the heavens amazed—it was as if the twenty dollar bill stopped in mid air—YES—it was as if the Lord stopped it in midair so I could see it clearly now—it was a $20.00!! It was falling in the area of the median of the Interstate, which meant that with the cars traveling so fast it would blow the bill all over the highway. Therefore, I ask the Lord to allow it to sit in one place and not move. He did exactly that, it sat there in the middle of I-4 traffic (cars traveling in excess of 70mph) and did not move. After the traffic cleared, I ran over to the median and picked it up; it was a newly issued twenty-dollar bill. As I came back to the car Linda had awoken and saw what was in my hand, and our friends stopped as well, but they did not see any money but what was in my hand.

> *Not that I am looking for a gift,*
> *but I am looking for*
> *what may be credited to your account.*
> *Philippians 4:17 KJV*

I had prayed—had faith—He provided for our needs with His infinite grace. Money does fall from the sky!!!!!!!!

This was a MIRACLE—TANGIBLE FAITH! As I drove back onto the highway in awe—I whispered another prayer. "Lord, thank you for this miracle please help us to be responsible and obedient to You that we may experience Your blessings!!!!!!!!!!"

> *And all these blessings shall come on thee, and*
> *overtake thee, if thou shalt hearken unto the*
> *voice of the LORD thy God.*
> *Deut 28:2 KJV*

The purpose of our life is to know God. Therefore, the focus of our life must be to seek God! To trust God, to put our faith in His Word, live by His commandments, focus our attention on Him, set our affections on things above—in other words, put God first and everything else will work out. The things we need will simply be added to us.

We had received a miracle—our jump-start. We would now begin our walk to the Promised Land. We would continue our focus on the Lord and let Him supply for our needs while we "sowed" a life of faith for Him – bringing glory to Him.

So begin to delight in God and watch His blessings come to you from every direction. As you take your attention off miracles, off your needs, and focus on God Himself, I believe you will begin to see blessings so big and numerous that you will not be able to comprehend them. God wants to bless you to overflowing so that you can be a living testimony of His goodness to in turn, bless others. When God is the center of your life, His goodness will displace worry and something wonderful will happen: You will enjoy a quality of life beyond miracles—life in the blessings of God! Amen.

In truth, whether or not we are enjoying the blessings of God is a better gauge of our walk with the Lord, because God's blessings are all conditional. There is always an "if."

If ye be willing and obedient,
ye shall eat the good of the land:
Isaiah 1:19 KJV

Miracles can come even when you are a unbeliever, but blessings require responsibility and obedience.

Jesus gave us the key to move into the life of blessings. In Matthew 6:25 he said,

Therefore I say unto you, Take no thought for
your life, what ye shall eat, or what ye shall
drink; nor yet for your body, what ye shall put
on. Is not the life more than meat, and the body
than raiment?

In other words, "Don't even think about it." Then He asks, "Is not the life more than meat, and the body than raiment." But what exactly is "the life?" He answers this question with – "But seek ye first the kingdom of God, and all these things shall be added unto you." Jesus defines "the life" as a fellowship with God.

When God blesses something, it multiplies. Now miracles are wonderful, but when the "miracle groceries" are gone, you are right back on your knees asking for another miracle! But, blessings are like seeds God places in our lives. His favor comes on everything we have and everything we put out our hand to do and multiplies it. If we really understand this, our prayer would be – "Oh God, don't give me miracles but give me blessings that keep producing after their own kind."

Al Coury

is a magician, motivational speaker, and conservationist. He believes everyone is responsible for contributing to a healthy, thriving planet where humanity and wildlife lives harmoniously. Al desires for our children and our children's, children to enjoy a clean and healthy world. He is an advocate for a clean planet and now ceased to represent companies he feel are not concerned about conservation and pollution. His only exception would be if he were doing a motivational speech explaining the ills of pollution and how many companies are going green and are still able to generate profits.

Al Coury was employed by IBM for 17 years and decided in 1985 to pursue a career as a magician full time. He as performed for: tradeshows, conventions and special events for such companies as; American Express, Morningstar, Mac Tools, BMW, White Rose, Mobile Oil Corp, Zeneca, Nordstrom, Mohawk, CitiCorp, DuPont, Natures Bounty, Cablevision Timeplex, Xerox, Mears, Turnstile Publishing, Ad2, Kellogg's, Drew Chemical, Belk Lindsey, Soiree Dignite, Miller, Space Labs, Sears, Florida Power, Midas, Roadway, Bonkerz Comedy Club, Manatee Festival, Ms. Orlando Beauty Pageant, Sagafjord (5 star cruise ship) DeBartolo Corporation, Hilton, Rosen, plus over 500 magic shows for the Westgate Resorts, and many others.

Multiple Streams of Success

Al's love for wildlife resulted in his performing for the Wildlife program in New York (Volunteers for Wildlife) where he put together and performed Magical Wildlife Shows using a rehabilitated owl, hawk, and other animals for many years. He was a teacher, counselor, and assistant director at Tannen's Magic Camp. He conferred with regarding the creation of a show utilizing magic for safety and substance abuse programs in the New York Metropolitan area. He has performed at over five hundred school assemblies; during three hundred of those, he used magic as a tool to explain the ills of drugs.

Contact information: al@alcourymagic.com

Follow Your Heart
But Use Your Head

Well, I may as well start at the beginning, and oh, what a beginning I had. I was an ugly baby. *How ugly were you?* Well, I was so ugly when I was born the doctor slapped my mother. My mother said, "What a treasure." My father said, "Yeah, let's bury it!"

As I got older, I got wiser, it was easier, my parents would take me on long rides out into the country, but I always surprised them and found my way back home. Seriously, the one Christmas I really remember was when I got my first two-wheel bicycle; it was a beat up, used bicycle with a flat tire. Oh, but I thought it was GOLD! It was the best Christmas present ever! I loved that bike. It was more than a bike. It was freedom. I could go out and explore, see sights, do things. It was wonderful!

The Laugh

I was always the skinny kid that everyone picked on in school. I would always be in trouble because I had this weird thing about me, whenever I was nervous I would laugh. So when anything happened I would be blamed. Someone would throw a spitball at the teacher, she would turn around, and the kids would point to me. I would start giggling, I would try to say it was not me but I would only laugh louder. When the school bully pushed me into a fight, we were sent to the principle's office. And, what do you think? The bully starts crying like there will be no tomorrow, saying that I started the fight, I am saying no, but of course, here goes the giggling. Now come on, this guy had to be two and a half times my size, but they believed him. To make matters worse, after school he starts telling everyone that I was the one crying like a little girl! That did not help my popularity.

I cannot tell you how many times I was grounded or when my old man hit me with the belt. All of this because of a laugh. Ok, sometimes I deserved it, like the time I put a tack under the cover of the chair where my mom normally sat. She sits and nothing. Oh well, I figured it must have slipped out. Well here comes, the old man, he never sat in that chair. You guessed it, this time he does. He howls like a banshee. Let me tell you, I could not sit for a week. It turns out my mom was wearing one of those old time girdles and a few layers of clothes so she never felt it. Why do those things always look so funny to kids when it is on TV?

Experimentation

My magic career started and ended at an early age, I was probably around eight or nine. I would save up some money and buy those little cheap tricks. One of them was the invisible ink, spray it on clothes and in less than a minute it would disappear. The old man had his buddies over to play cards. I went over to one of his friends and said, "Look at my new pen." Then of course, I squirted it all over his white shirt. Before I could say anything my old man whacked me so hard I went flying, then he started kicking me. Yes, he really kicked me. His friends were pulling him off me saying, "Look! Look! It's only a trick. The ink disappeared." Well, it did not matter. Besides that beating, I was punished for a week and that is when I said no more tricks for me.

Finally, I made it to high school, but I was still being picked on. Books knocked out of my hands, pushed, punched even spit on, harassed to no end, both mentally and physically. My Mom would always say, "Turn the other cheek." However, that never worked. I would just be hit on that side, too! I finally was fed up and decided that if I did not do something about this it was never going to change and only get worse.

I saved up my money and bought a set of weights. I started drinking as many thick shakes as I could and ate like there was no tomorrow. I would go out and get anything that was advertised to put on muscle or weight. I bought a book on self-defense, sewed a bunch of old clothes together, and stuffed them so I could practice on a full size dummy. I worked out two, three, sometimes four hours almost every day.

I put on over thirty pounds in less than a year. I was still slim, being 5' 10" and weighing 140 pounds. But, boy, did I have muscle—27-inch waist and a 41-inch chest! (Hey, Bruce Lee was only 130 pounds, and you would not want to mess with him.) Most of this I did over summer vacation so when I went back to school I was a changed man.

Yep, I was no more a boy. The best part was there were four guys that picked on me the most. (Well, actually, there were two best parts. The girls were starting to notice me.) Well, were they in for a surprise!

The first one, Mike started picking on me on the school bus. Of course, I said, "Leave me alone!" as I did a hundred times. He said, "Oh, yeah! What ya gonna do about it!" like he said a hundred times. But, this time I said, "Wait 'til we get off the bus and I'll show you," And, of course, the entire bus full of kids went "Ohhhhhh!" and started yelling "Fight! Fight! Fight!" He started laughing and said I was really going to get it this time and maybe I should call my mommy and other things I could not put in print. You know how high school boys can be. By the way, this was an all boy high school, so of course with no girls around, these guys had a lot more frustration built up and were dying for an outlet, like a good old-fashioned fight.

Now, Mike was a big guy, stood almost a head higher than I was, that is why they called him Big Mike. We get off the bus—so do about half the kids. The bus was stopped for a red light so the rest of the kids could see what unfolded. They were all yelling and screaming and egging Mike on, except Mike did not need any egging. Big Mike finally throws a punch at my face; I caught his punch mid air with my left hand. No one expected me to do that! I'll never forget it was like everything was going in slow motion except for me, I sure wont forget the look on his face. I smiled and shot a few rapid punches to his face with my right and then a

132

couple to his stomach and he just crumpled to the floor, never having laid a finger on me.

The crowd went wild! They were yelling, "Hit him again! Kick him!" Boy, they were out for blood. But, I had proved my point. I am sure the humility was much worse than the beating I gave him. I just walked away the proudest that I had ever been in my life.

The next guy was just as big, if not bigger, and a lot stronger. One day in school, he starts picking on me and he said that after school he was going to kick my butt. He was going to smear me all over the street. After school, we get into it. Wow, what a fight it was! It went up and down the street. It was like one of those old John Wayne movies. It went on and on. Finally, at one of those lulls, that break in the fight, where both guys come up for air, I said, that is it, I had enough. I turned my back and started to walk away and he punches me in the back. I spun around, smashed him in the face, and hammered him with a bunch of lefts and rights as I screamed out some not so nice words. I said, "I had enough, you got a problem with that!" He was holding his face and just kind of shook his head and backed away. I consider that fight a draw, but he never ever bothered me again.

The third guy was easy to deal with. I was walking through the park where everyone hung out. Someone called me over. There were about a dozen or so guys and girls hanging out. When I got closer I could see that one in particular was the creep who really loved taunting me. He got a real kick out of picking on me, especially in front of the girls. He was sitting at one of the concrete chess tables. I knew he was not going to play chess; he wanted to show off to the girls. Well, some of the guys were arm wrestling, and of course, they would love to pick on me because I was such an easy target. Well, up to that point I was.

So of course, he starts to egg me into arm wrestling with him. I made as if I did not want to, but on the inside, I was dying to fight him. Finally, I agreed and sat down at the table with him; I let him take my arm about three quarters of the way down and then stopped! You should have seen the look on his face! He is huffing and puffing and I just nonchalantly pushed his arm over to the other side and then slammed it down. Well, just like the first bully, he never picked on me again.

One day, as I got on the bus, the last one of the bullies saw me get and he ran off the back! I ran off the bus in pursuit. I chased him for blocks, but he had too

Multiple Streams of Success

much of a head start. However, seeing him run like that and all of his friends seeing him run from me was satisfying enough for me.

After that, I still got into some fights, but I never started one unless I saw someone being picked on. That would make my blood boil! It did not matter who it was or where it was, if I saw someone getting picked on, I would stand up for him or her. I guess I could just have easily have turned into a "bad ass," but then I would have been exactly what I detested the most, a bully.

Things got much better; I started dating, having real friends, and really enjoying myself. But, then I did a stupid thing. Yep. I got the girlfriend pregnant! So all in one year I got married, had a child, got divorced, and graduated from high school. What a year!

At least my son turned out to be great; he has a good head on his shoulders and is down to earth with many accomplishments. I am very proud of him. I had to move back home for a while, in-between jobs—just hanging around.

Kicked Out

Ha, but that did not last my Mom said, "Get a job or get out!" Of course, I said, "But, no one wants to hire me!" Then she opened up a newspaper and said,

"Look IBM is hiring customer engineers." I replied, "I have no idea what a customer engineer is." Mom said it did not matter, go down there and get an interview. I went down and applied, took an aptitude test. I scored really high thanks to the fact that my high school was a trade school, meaning that I took four extra periods of shop for four years and my major was electronics.

When they hired me, they told me I was the youngest one hired in that division. During my eleventh year with IBM, I was hanging out with one of my fellow engineers; his name was Hector, a real nice fellow. I did not know that Hector was an amateur magician and a great one at that. We were hanging out at this club and he starts doing some magic for some ladies we met. These girls were going crazy, they were laughing one minute and completely amazed the next. Everyone was having a great time, coins melted from one hand to the other, fantastic wild card tricks, and the best, taking a lit cigarette, placing it lit into a handkerchief and it disappeared right before everyone's eyes and the smoke just drifting away, it's still is in my repertoire and one of my favorites.

Developing a Passion
Wow, I was blown away! I had to beg him

almost every day for six months, "Please teach me magic!" He finally broke down and agreed. He started by showing me something extremely difficult, but, I did not know any better. I worked on this one trick for months and finally one day Hector said let me show you something easier. I said, "Why did you show me something so hard when this other stuff is much easier?" He said, "Well, I just wanted to make sure you were sincere at learning magic for magic's sake and not just to show off."

I guess, originally, it was just to impress the ladies, but it grew on me. I wanted to learn magic for the art form it is. I guess when I was younger and started my practical jokes it was to make people laugh. But, now I can elicit all types of responses there is laughter, amazement, wonder and best of all its entertainment, its fun. I am a kid who never grew up and I make other people feel like kids again. At the very least, I bring a smile to their face and a bit of that magical wonder we experienced as a child.

It turned out I really had a knack for magic. I might have been a late bloomer, being that most magicians I speak to have been doing it since early childhood. I started when I was thirty years old. But, I really put my heart and soul into it. I would practice for hours and hours, day after day, week after week, month after month. At the beginning my hands would actually be bruised and, on more than one occasion, bloody.

However, I kept at it! It finally paid off. To gain entrance to "Ring 244 the Frank Garcia Ring" a fantastic magic club in Long Island New York, the requirement was to perform first for the officers of the magic club. If you passed that preliminary test, then you were to perform for the whole club. The members would then vote whether you were in or out. Well, I passed both auditions with no problem, but what I did not know was that in the audience was the owner for a New York entertainment agency by the name of "Enchanted Parties." It turned out Marty was an amateur magician.

Going Pro

After my presentation, Marty approached me and asked me if I would be interested in working for his entertainment company. He told me he was looking for someone with skill and personality, upbeat and could make people feel comfortable and deliver lots of laughs. I was not too sure until he told me what he wanted to pay me. Ow, I almost fell over. It was a no brainier. I guess all that practicing and being a practical joker finally paid off. Think of it, I used to get in trouble for my practical jokes now I get paid for making people laugh!

Magical Mistake

Ok, I do not pull practical jokes on my clients, but my poor (wonderful and amazing) girlfriend Jennifer and my other friends had better watch out. Case in point, picture a kitchen table, the kind that separates in the middle so you can add a leaf and make the table longer. I separated the table, took a piece of cardboard the same width as table and cut a hole big enough for my head to fit in, took a tablecloth and cut a hole in it to match. Got a cardboard box slightly bigger than my head, left the bottom open and covered it with wrapping paper. That went on top of the table with all the holes lined up. I put a note by the front door telling my dear Jennifer that I had to run over to my neighbor's house and help him but I had left her a little something on the kitchen table. Of course, I put a video camera in the cupboard, taped over the red light, and pointed it at the table.

When I saw her pull into the driveway, I turned on the camera, jumped under the table, and put my head in the box. She came in, read the note, and says aloud, "Ohhhh, my honey left me a present." She walked over to the table and grabbed the box, but instead of picking up the box, she tried to pull it to the front of the table. Here is my head in the box bouncing back and forth, bam, bam, bam, ouch, ouch, ouch. Finally, she lifts up the box and I say "Hi, honey!" Well, she screamed, knocked over the little island butcher block, knocked over the chairs, knocked over everything in her path. She went flying out of the room, realizes what just happened, stopped in the middle of the living room, came back into the kitchen, and kicked my butt. Yeah, but it was worth it!

Magic All the Time

Eventually I left IBM and started doing magic full-time. Skill, personality, and a bit of luck paid off. I should add that although people outside the magic community, people that I did magic for, whether paying clients or non-magic friends, were always saying I should do magic for a living. I thought they were just being nice, giving me a compliment, because when I asked the magicians in the clubs I belonged to most of them said, "What, are you crazy? You cannot make a living doing magic." It took me a while to realize that what they were actually saying was that they could not make a living at magic. I decided to follow my heart, and boy am I happy. Magic has been great to me; it is always fun and always a challenge.

Marty, affectionately called Uncle Marty by everyone who knows him, calls me up one day and says he has a client who is looking for a magician to do some of his trade shows. The company was also a fundraising company that worked with schools. The company's idea was to send me into the schools to excite the kids into selling his products.

I am sure some child has rung your doorbell or one of your friends or associates has had their child come to you to purchase from them some cookies, books, wrapping paper, cooking utensils, the list goes on and on. The money goes to some school project or outing. I had a meeting with the fellow in charge; I became very interested in his concept. I started throwing some ides around and it turned into a full-blown brainstorming session. I came up with the idea of two shows. The one for the younger children leaned more towards safety issues (do not talk to strangers; look both ways when you cross the street, etc.). For the older children it was a "Just say no to drugs" theme. I would incorporate the message into the magic. I did not know the psychology behind it at the time, but I did know it would deliver the message much, much better than some boring lecture. Kids always hear "do not do this," "do not do that," and eventually it just goes in one ear and out the other. However, with the magic delivering the message, they are listening more and absorbing more of the message.

I understand now because I have studied the psychology and science of how our senses work. We have five senses, the more of the senses that we use while learning something new the more likely we are to recall something. Case in point: You see a picture of a lion. Okay, it is impressive. After all, he is the king of the jungle. However, it is only a picture, Now what happens if you see a real lion? Much more impressive! Then you get close enough to smell the lion. How about, if after that, you stand next to him and you actually touch him? How about being able to wrap your arms around him? What happens if he licks you? (Better, hope he is not hungry.)

The picture of the lion stays in your mind a few hours, maybe a day. Seeing him lasted you all week. Seeing and smelling him could actually last for years, whenever you smell something similar you would say, "Oh, yeah, I remember that great lion." In addition, whenever you touched something furry you would probably think about that magnificent lion. (I will not even get into the licking part; I just hope you would not run when your significant other tries to kiss you.) Therefore, the more senses involved, the more sensory input, the more significant, the more impressive something is, the longer it will remain in your memory. I remember the bicycle, I remember the bullies, and I remembered the magic.

So, if I were to lecture kids about drugs without the magic, they would probably be thinking of what they would be doing after school. Their mind some were else, just giving the semblance of being there. However, if the magic delivers the message: picture this, I blow up a balloon and hand it to a child (they are part of the magic) everyone in that general area feels a part of it too. I take a two-foot long, big, sharp knitting needle with a few feet of yarn (the kind that they use for making sweaters) dangling from the end of it. I slam the needle against the table; they hear the metal hit the table all the way at the back of the room.

I talk about making believe the balloon is their brain, the needle represents the drugs. I then say "The pusher, the person who gives or sells you the drugs will say, 'Look it won't hurt you." I push the big needle into the balloon and out the other side. The balloon does not burst. I then say, "Well, sometimes you don't realize that the drug is slowly killing you." I then show the balloon all around and then I pull the needle out the opposite end, so now the yarn is running through it and throw the balloon. (So try to picture this I have just pushed the needle threw the balloon, the yarn is going through the balloon, and is dangling a couple of feet behind the needle).

I'm holding the needle pulling the balloon around, walking out into the audience letting some children touch the balloon or yarn as I say, "The pusher, the person who gave you the drug, is saying 'See I told you there is nothing to worry about.' But, you know it's not true, eventually the drugs will catch up with your mind, will catch up with your brain and then. . ." I take the needle and poke the balloon and it bursts with a real loud pop. I add, "So, the pusher, the person who sells or gives you the drugs, doesn't care about you. He only cares about your money making its way into his pocket. Where do you want to keep your money? Your pocket or his?" The kids always yell out, "My pocket!" So, instead of a boring lecture, they get involved, they are entertained, they talk about the magic and are reminded of the message. More sensory input the longer the message remains.

I have performed over more than three-hundred magic safety shows and magic "Say No to Drugs" programs in about two and one half years. In addition, I was the first one to do it in the New York area. One thing about children is that their job in life is to catch the magician! They will always keep you on your toes, if you can really entertain and fool children and enjoy doing it, then you can entertain anyone. They say that working comedy clubs is tough, I found it to be a piece of cake compared to a children's show. Weddings, bar & bat mitzvahs, cruise ship, house parties, and corporate events are all a piece of cake compared to a children's show.

That is, if the children's show is done right. Meaning your energy level has to be higher than their's. Getting them wild and crazy but always controlling the situation. I really hate the boring kids' magician that gets up and says these are the rules we are going to follow, and no yelling, no getting out of your seats, no this, and no that. BORING! Hey, it is a birthday party, where kids should be kids, get them excited!

When I finish a children's show I go home, take a shower, and then take a nice long nap because I am totally worn out. It is a workout, and just like a regular workout, it is worth it. But, it is also always full of fun surprises. I do this one trick with a ten-inch square bag, two children help me examine the "empty" bag. I ask the little boy, maybe five years old, to act like a chicken. Then I ask the little girl to reach inside the bag. She reaches inside the bag. Lo and behold—she pulls out a huge chicken egg. I say to the little fellow, "My gosh, you laid an egg!" One time this little boy grabs the egg from the girl thinking that he just laid the egg. With his eyes wide open he says, "Let me hatch it!" He proceeds to sit on the floor with the egg underneath him acting like a chicken! The crowd went berserk, hysterical with laughter. Telling you does not do it justice, you really had to be there. I bet I had done that trick hundreds of times and never had a child do that before. Kids are always full of surprises.

Now, some magicians refuse to do children shows, I always wondered if maybe the children figured out the magic or maybe the magicians cannot keep up with the energy level of the children. How can a magician call him or herself a magician and not enjoy doing children's shows?

On the other hand, some magicians do the corporate market and do not do children's shows because they do not want that type of image. I do not agree with that philosophy. Hey, to each his own! Although most of my work is trade shows and corporate magic, I still enjoy doing children shows. You can learn a lot from children. You can learn how to deliver a message, how to keep someone's attention, and, especially, how to entertain all ages.

Most people believe that children have a short attention span; I believe they are looking for information overload. Meaning they want to do twelve different things at the same time. They are these huge sponges. They are a like a black hole in outer space sucking in all this information. They are not trying to catch the magician to embarrass him/her but to show that they have figured out or solved what is being presented.

They love real magic, but at the same time, they are looking at the challenge of trying to "catch the magician." They are developing their problem solving skills; it is part of their learning process. To hold children's attention there has to be something that drives them, their favorite hobby, game, sport etc., or in this case really good entertaining magic. Let me tell you, when a child comes up to me and says, "Boy, you are a real magician." then I know I am. I learned how to deliver a message through magic for children. Then doing a trade show incorporating the client's product/message was relatively simple.

Trade Show Magic

Presenting the message on the trade show floor is a different manner. When people go to see a magic show or any type of show for that manner, they go to the venue were it is being held, they take their seats and know what they are there for, to be entertained. They are looking to have a great time, they are anticipating a great time.

Those people are rooting for you before you even get on stage. Not to be able to entertain people in that type of venue means you might want to think about a career change. However, at a trade show people are there to see all the latest gadgets, or find the best product or service for their home or company. Talk about information overload! Hundreds, usually thousands of people going up and down the aisles and dozens if not hundreds of companies trying to get them to not only stop at their booth but to purchase their product or service, at the very least remember them.

The average tradeshow booth is ten feet long; a company has about two to three seconds to catch a prospects attention as they walk by their booth. Enter the dragon, well the Trade Show Magician anyway! A really good tradeshow magician, or a great one like myself (Well come on, I have to toot my own horn a little!), will maximize the effectiveness of an exhibit. My job is to make attendees see, remember, and to better recognize the companies name and product. People lose 40 % of what is said within twenty minutes, 60 % within six hours, and a whopping 90 % within one week. That is unless you have a hook, something to remind them of the product.

Possibly, they see a coin, a pack of cards, a rope, or a flame—what do they think? "Hey remember that magician at XYZ Company!" Remember what I said earlier about presenting magic with a message was a different animal at a tradeshow? Most magicians fall on their face at a tradeshow. This is not like the show I mentioned above. There is no captive audience. There are people walking helter-skelter, back and forth. Some are on a mission. Some are extremely tired from all the walking and the sensory overload. Some have the trade show gaze. Some do not even remember why they are there. Some wish they did not have to be there.

The tradeshow magician knows how to pull attendees into the booth, get them to relax, catch their breath, and have a great time. Through the magic, they hear the name of the company and understand the product in a no-pressure way that is more relaxed, more open, and more fun. Sure makes the sales person's job much easier!

Motivationally Speaking

Motivational speaking came about mostly because of the extreme difference in the service I experienced with two different companies. One was the exceptional service that I received from Eureka Vacuum Company and the other was the utter lack of customer service from Rheem Air Conditioner. Let us start with the exceptional service. It has been quite a few years ago but, I had a Eureka Vacuum Cleaner. One day I was using the vacuum, shut it off, and when I went to turn it back on it would not work. I called the help line, and guess what? I got a real live person who knew what they were talking about. I told him the problem, we tried a few things, but it would not work. He said I would have to send it back to the company, but upon checking the warranty dates, discovered that it had expired five weeks prior. During our conversation, I explained to him I hardly used the vacuum cleaner and I was disappointed that it did not hold up any better. Well, I could not believe my ears. He said, "Al, I will tell you what, UPS it to us. If we see that, as you say, it has hardly been used we will fix it at no cost to you. If we feel it has had regular use we will give you an estimate. Either way we will send it back to you by UPS at no charge."

I sent it back and honestly thought they would just send me a letter saying, "it will cost you x dollars." But, lo and behold, within a few days, he personally calls me back and says, "You're right, Al. It has hardly been used; we are sending it back and have even upgraded it at no cost. Can you believe that? Wow! I thought that he and his company really cared about customer service. And of course, they have a customer for life and of course, I tell everyone about their exceptional service. I even have gone so far as to go down the aisle where department stores sell vacuum cleaners and if I see someone shopping for one I will tell them of my experience with Eureka. I have probably sold more vacuums then the salespeople there. Ha ha.

Now for the not so good experience with Rheem. While still under warranty, the air conditioner/heater stopped working. The same company that installed it came to repair it. Yep, they said, "the compressor died, but it is under warranty." They said I would only have to pay for the labor. I thought, "Okay, that was understandable." Until I got the bill, that is. Then I almost fell on the floor. I said to the repairman, "Excuse me. But you said I would be charged for labor. How is it that I am charged for gas and all these other parts?" Well, you probably have been in that situation; it is the old "got you over the barrel situation." I then talked to the boss, and of course, I got the old run around. His boss told me to call Rheem and of course when I called I was switched around, disconnected, sent to the wrong department, could not get the right person, most of the time could not even get a person. I then wrote letters. What really infuriated me the most was the fact that they did not give me the courtesy of a call, but that they sent me a form letter excluding any of the complaints I filed with them.

Thinking Outside the Box

So, what is a person to do? Well, if you are a magician that knows how to incorporate a message with the magic and you are used to speaking to people, why not become a motivational speaker? So *Thinking Outside the Box* and *Customer Service* were born.

All I have to say is these are the facts, not embellished in any way, actually toned down because of limited space. You be the judge, I know I will have a Eureka in my closet for life.

It is a fact that every person has the potential to reach at least two hundred people; family, friends, people at work, churches, clubs etc. I am sure you have gotten the point, be the best you can be, show compassion, have good business sense, but make sure you have people sense because that is what keeps your business alive.

I hope you see all the steps that were taken, all the trails followed. There was no school to go to, to learn what I learned except the school of hard knocks! I believe a person has to keep a very open mind. There are so many experts out there but most of them contradict each other. Why called them experts when they cannot even agree on the same topic, especially when all it takes is a little common sense. I guess what I am trying to say is the heck with the experts, it is only their opinion, and then they get to put their degree after it.

Therefore, whatever your dreams, your desires, keep an open mind—think outside the box. Listen to what people or the experts have to say, sort thru all the information, make your best judgment call after carefully considering all the options. Use your own common sense, your own observations. Take and ask for constructive criticism from people you can trust to tell you the truth. And, when experts or associates, family or friends say you cannot do something, think outside the box. Follow your heart but use your head. Believe in your self!

By the way, did I mention that I did all this with a head injury from a head-on motorcycle accident that left me with fragmented memory? Guess I forgot that part. Have a magical life...

Dr. Phyllis M Olmstead

is an international speaker and author. She has lectured on education, technology, and distance education on five continents. She is published worldwide. Dr Olmstead obtained her bachelor degree in Agribusiness and Natural Resources Education at the University of Florida, a master's degree in Vocational Administration and a doctoral degree in Curriculum and Instruction from the University of Central Florida.

Dr Olmstead, a Rotary Paul Harris Fellow, has a service mentality and works with the American Cancer Society's Relay for Life, has a Relay for Life team, is a trained American Cancer Society Triple Touch II instructor, the local Mission Education Chair for Relay for Life, trained in patient services, and is a legacy member of ACS. She has recently been nominated for the prestigious Summit Award.

Dr O is a board of director of Habitat for Humanity of Greater Apopka and is a legacy member of the Affiliate. Additionally, she is a Heritage member of Canine Companions for Independence, is on the board of directors of The Daisy House in Apopka, and partner's with many schools in the community. She is also a board member of Health Masters Club, a nonprofit organization designed to assist children in developing healthy lifestyles. Olmstead is an Ambassador for the Chamber of Commerce of Greater Apopka and is both a business and personal lifetime member of the Apopka Historical Society. She is a

Multiple Streams of Success

booster of the Veterans of Foreign Wars Post 10147 in Apopka. Dr O is a legacy member of Hospice of the Comforter in honor of her late husband, Jeffery.

Dr O is a businessperson with a thriving shipping and printing franchise and she privately owns a publishing company. Olmstead has taught public middle and high school and has been in both administration and instruction at an international distance education university headquartered in Florida. She has taught students all over the third rock from the sun.

Contact information: phyllis@olmstead.com

Can I Motivate You?

"Aspire to Inspire Before You Expire"

Church Marquee Zellwood, FL

How do you inspire people to seek their own level of perfection? How do you get them to be the best that they can be?

Setting a person up for success is so much easier than setting her/im up for failure. Inspire people by letting them know that they ARE capable, that they CAN and WILL achieve.

As an educator, I entered the classroom (some with walls and some without) and informed my students that they all had an 'A' grade right then. . . individually each one determined if s/he maintained an 'A' or if s/he didn't. This philosophy not only started the course off on a positive note, but also allowed each student to determine her/is destiny in the program.

Give those you mentor high standards and hold yourself to similar heights. It is possible that you are the only person who will be a positive role model in their lives. Encourage your mentees to read about other role models and suggest movies of true-life courageous people so they may expand their definitions of success, strength, tenacity, and perseverance.

Being A Catalyst

Some young people have minimal self-worth due to familial or environmental conditions. It often took small steps to inspire these students to achieve anything. For example, my first teaching experience was in a small rural area in South Central Florida. There were two traffic lights where the town was bisected by a state road and the lights turned to flashing after 6:00 pm each day. Everyone there knew each other and there was only a weekly paper in the community.

One day I opened the paper and read that two unnamed boys were arrested breaking into the junior high school and for stealing a lawnmower. I told my new husband, "Drats! L. P. will miss school again tomorrow!" (He was already being pulled out of my class weekly by a probation officer.) My husband asked, "How do you know the child was L. P.?" Well, in a town that small, with one high school and one pool of possible suspects, you just knew. Sure enough, the next day I discovered that L. P. missing school and in jail.

I taught Agriculture and Natural Resources Education at the school and L. P. was in my ninth grade program. He was among 32 students who had been "administratively placed" into the high school with all failing grades for their three years of junior high.

The retiring guidance counselor placed all of them in the vocational agriculture program so they wouldn't disturb and hold back other programs, after all "Agriculture is just pulling weeds and doesn't require any reading or writing." I taught my students gardening, welding, small engine repair, animal husbandry, citrus production, business management, public speaking, and other rural agribusiness related skills—all requiring reading, writing, safety skills, and thinking.

I remember L. P. carefully planting and caring for the precious 200 square feet of garden allotted him. One day another boy in the class stepped into L.P.'s plot of well-groomed vegetables. L. P. was so upset about this indiscretion that he body slammed the other student to the ground destroying all his own hard work. He let his rage take over resulting in the total obliteration of months of hard work of which he was so proud. His low self-esteem and poor adult life models surfaced suddenly, undermining his success again.

Multiple Streams of Success

After leaving that county at the end of the school year, I moved to Orange County, FL, and a few years later returned to my childhood stomping grounds in Lakeland, FL, one holiday to shop. The Sheriff's Boys Ranch happened to be located there in Polk County and L. P. had spent the rest of his youth there. I was walking through the mall when this handsome gangly young man walked directly towards me and gave me an incredible bear hug. He declared, "Miss Pirkle, you changed my life! I have stayed straight, got out of the Boy's Ranch and have a small engine repair business [making more money than I did]. It was all because of you! If you had not shown me how to fix lawn mower engines I would have never known I had a talent for mechanics and would still be stealing lawnmowers instead of fixing them. I would probably be in prison right now!" What a blessing to see how my life has impacted the life on a developing human being, seeing him progress from being a "burden on society" to full fledged taxpaying hard working individual!

In Orange County, FL, I taught agriculture in an urban middle school with students from all socioeconomic strata. Because the students were placed in elective courses on an exploratory wheel system, the students were mixed by academic and socioeconomic status in each class. Often the most disruptive students were the ones that struggled to succeed academically and socially. One day while I was walking through the halls of the social studies wing, a young woman, who was normally very disruptive and challenging to teach, squealed, "Mrs. Olmstead, I love you!" and gave me a great big hug. "What was that for?" I asked. She said her history teacher had just handed her a report card and that I had "given" her her first passing grade in three years. Without taking a breath I replied, "I don't 'give' grades to anyone. You earned that 'D' on your own. If you had earned an 'F' or an 'A' I would have reported that, also." This small success turned around her attitude in my class and she proved to herself she could achieve, if only in my classroom. That was almost 20 years ago, I hope she has continued to develop her self-worth and achieve something in her life that has helped mankind.

Being A Model

My youth was filled with great examples of service and personal strength. Although I was raised on a farm where we made our own clothes, grew our own crops, raised our own beef, rabbit, poultry, and pork, and canned our own food, I saw examples of giving everyday.

We would give extra crops to the widow who lived at the edge of our dairy farm, we would split a steer we slaughtered with other relatives, we all joined in on building projects and gathering hay no matter whose cattle it was for, and we made blankets and clothes for babies that were on the way. At a community level, we were sure to put coins in the Alms for the Poor box hanging at the exit of the church, we would go caroling at the nursing home and hospital, and we made goodie baskets at Easter, Mother's Day, and Father's Day for the residents who had no families to visit them. The most poignant of memories of giving through acts of the Girl Scouts, school, and 4-H was those of making 'ditty bags' for the soldiers serving in Viet Nam. We would sew together washcloths into a drawstring bag then fill the usable bags with cakes of soap, safety razors, toothpaste, toothbrushes, deodorant, and other little things that were sorely missed by the soldiers in the rice paddies and jungles of Southeast Asia.

As a prominent role model in my community, I make sure that all my efforts are guided toward service of others. I encourage customers of my store to donate their time and talents to local charities, such as, Relay for Life of the American Cancer Society, Habitat for Humanity of Greater Apopka, Canine Companions for Independence, the Daisy House, or Camp Thunderbird for the developmentally disabled.

I use space that I pay for in my business review articles and advertisements in the local newspapers to support these and other causes. Signs posted in my store offer support for these charities and literature for those needing assistance from the programs. I encourage each business that I deal with and author that I publish to offer a percentage of their income to support a cause of great importance to her/is heart. As the motto of Rotary International states, I believe in "Service Above Self." I am here to serve my neighbors and those throughout the world with my both my time, talents, and funds, of which I am so fortunate to be blessed.

Being Grateful

At the end of every shift when my employees say good-bye or at the end of the pay period, I try to say "Thank you," "It was a good day," or at least, "You tried hard today." I personally have had many employers in the past who have never complimented or thanked me for my hard work. One said, "Your paycheck is thanks enough, you ought to be thanking me for letting you have a job." I have often said to students and teachers that sometimes you get a job "to learn how not to be a good boss."

A supervisor at a distance education university I worked for gave me a negative comment on my evaluation for "not completing the job within the 40 hour work week" for all the extra time I put in polishing work and helping colleagues with publication and websites. I could not understand this after coming from the public school culture where we were expected to work late and take grading and planning home with us. Even though he was an administrator and professor, my supervisor stuck to his 40 hours and I felt that he was saying that either I was inefficient in performing my tasks or just trying to show him up by being the first one on campus and the last one to leave.

This was a difficult transition for me from dedicating my life to my work (read "workaholic") to only "putting in my forty." Fortunately, his 40-hour workweek policy was not a consistent practice on campus. Many other administrators and professors went above and beyond the expectations of their job descriptions to meet more fully the needs of our students.

One day, the Provost of the college unapologetically made a 7:00 am appointment with me because he knew I would be there before he would. In addition, the Provost always walked around and greeted everyone each day, thanked her/him for a great job or for positive feedback received from a student. He offered cash and a trophy as bonus incentive plans or "extrinsic rewards" for innovative ideas and encouraged collaboration instead of isolation when conducting projects and writing grants. He would give out the quarterly BIPs at campus-wide parties and encouraged each of his deans to reward regularly their direct reports with similar incentive rewards to encourage excellent and above average work ethics. The Provost even asked me to collaborate with him on a publishing venture that continued for almost a decade, long past the end of his 25-year tenure at the school.

Being A Mentor

My mentor, Kathleen "Miss Kitty" Harrell, is an octogenarian now. She was a fantastic 4-H leader in Polk County who lead us to excel in every project we attempted. She was unable to have children herself and

Multiple Streams of Success

spent most of her youth in a Catholic orphanage, but went on to mother me and countless other young people over the years. I remember her constant organization of club meetings, contests, speaking activities, Toastmaster programs, and individual learning sessions. She inspired, directed, drove, fed, and nurtured us to do our best at everything we attempted, be it sewing, cooking, gardening, public speaking, modeling, leadership, organizational management, writing, making radio and newspaper public announcements, or just singing at the local nursing home during the holidays.

Inspiring self-sacrifice and public service were two of the strongest characteristics she inspired in me. I then have tried to inspire these characteristics in the students and teachers I have educated over the years.

Robin Andre Rodrigue

is a native of New Orleans and honors English graduate of the University of Florida, Robin Rodriguez began his career in renovation of French Quarter properties and management. In recent years, he has dedicated himself to writing and to being of service to others. He attends the Fathers House Christian Center. Robin lives in Florida with his four cats.

Contact information: robrodrigue@yahoo.com

Rasselas Revisited

My first nine years were passed in French Louisiana and Lafourche Parish specifically, scavenging banks of murky bayous, pilfering stalks of sugar cane for kid manufactured sweets and roaming swamps for mystifying aquatic life-forms, whose existence fired Cajun cuisine. This mythscape gave life, and along with the local tribe I gave praise to gods of food, drink and carnival, stern old men at a control panel, I imagined, unlike the nice guy consumed on Sunday. The French supplanted the American, the old world the new, with Catholic and Pagan ritual flourishing side by side. My grandfather exorcised a wart on my hand with potato juice, all the while chanting to dawn's moon; the priest exorcised my sins. For years after I suspected a dermatologic property common to spuds, a fallacy inherent to intercession. Reason had no part in fashioning happenstance; passion, rite and enchantment furnished all means to direct life; and one's life depended on never antagonizing the pantheon of local deities, lest glorified he or she render every fell bane. Such was the life, drifting euphorically among the surreal and Bacchian, and I wanted to live there forever. My parents longed to live elsewhere, and purchased an old, wrecked apartment building in New Orleans' French Quarter. In 1971 we moved into the same, unwitting sacrifices all to the gods of New Babylon.

My story begins in the *Vieux Carre*, long home to writers and otherwise strangers in an estranged land, detached and intimate with the prevailing unreal and all too real. My journey, a writer's journey, followed just this pathway, commencing in unreality and evolving to the mystery that is reality. I was the contemptuous son of an abusive father, a man whose inner demons thundered in outward abuse. An aerospace engineer by trade, he and thousands like him went unemployed with the seventies' dip in defense spending. Rage set in with pressures of a mortgage, derelict property, peeved wife, five kids, hounding creditors and no greenbacks. I've wondered if his generation's disposition for ragging on children came from their bombing of foreign peoples. However gotten, the sixties and seventies saw unrestrained domestic violence, and I became devastated recipient of physical, verbal and mostly emotional abuse. So many individuals shirk self-determination for popular determination. With problems at home came

170

problems at school and elsewhere as others enlisted in a malevolent crusade. Following years of everywhere condemnation I sank into drug induced confusion and committed my greatest error to date, accepting the curses leveled on me, believing and living them.

Life comes from death. From dark years I took an immeasurable treasure of incomparable significance, so prized I know no less than providence intended my trying journey. In Samuel Johnson's *Rasselas* the story's protagonist deserts an Eden-like paradise and journeys through Western thought. He meets the Epicurean, Stoic and man of science, among others, but finds everywhere suffering, an allegory for the Western experience since the Biblical Fall. I too journeyed through mental space, beginning in innocence, progressing to a fall and suffering and climaxing with a deeper awareness of a fallen and suffering world. Observing the destructive personalities of my early life, I learned how they engendered doom and how to avoid it, realized prevailing objective truths govern life with subjective thought influencing it, and understood reality is created in consciousness.

Everything begins with perception. We interpret people, places and things in terms of duality: Good-bad, white-black, plus-minus. Processing sensory perception, the mind converts that data into belief and we act on it. Painful experience—a black—colors our beliefs in gloomy shades, which in turn influences behavior. Perception shapes beliefs; beliefs determine thoughts and actions. In my youth and beyond I suffered innumerable bad experiences, which dyed my life in the darkest hues. With age and understanding I reinterpreted former blacks: Invaluable lessons were learned, a deeper awareness of life gained. In every way I garnered insight through hardship never grasped in contentment. Blacks are less black and more white, green, blue and lavender. People overlook the color spectrum and otherwise reality behind pretense because they don't know to look for it.

Secular philosophy offers an interesting interpretation of the Biblical Fall. The Fall began not with an apple but when God created Eve. Knowledge of good and evil came into the world. Duality came into the world. The first parents saw black and white, good and bad, but their perception had no reality outside consciousness. Either they missed yellows, greens and blues, or relegated them to the dual categories, effectively buying into a false reality. The world East of

Eden got smaller because those perceiving it lacked the perception to comprehend its magnitude. My world— my reality—as those of others I knew diminished for the same reason. I came to see through the spell, having long heard preposterous explanations to account for me, and coming thereby to question perception, misperception and their relationship to reality. With deepening awareness I pondered if anything bad happened to me given greater understanding gained. Others I knew never saw the color spectrum, dwelling in a black and white phenomenal plane removed from all meaning. Their blacks were pitch black and dreadful. Without mine I would be a barren palette, sketching a colorless reality confined by my imagination or lack of it. Hidden meaning underlies misfortune. Such is the overlooked reality of our lives.

Earlier I posited perception shapes belief, but in truth the misperception of early years warps belief, which then blinds perception. The old adage has it seeing is believing; in truth, believing is seeing. In my life, of course, I was told the worse and believed it, becoming a self-fulfilling prophecy of a doomed vision told to me and accepted by me. Restrained or untrammeled, one's view on the world stems from his or her beliefs about it, and for everyone clear sight demands suspension of belief. A man I knew went into everything expecting to see something, and perceived very little. I go into everything expecting to see nothing, and perceive a great deal. I learned never to restrict my perception with preconceived notions. For years others advanced laughable commentary on me, noting all my failures and none of my triumphs, denying themselves any good I offered. We see what we want to see, not what's actually there, and miss opportunities because we can't clear our own heads. Intangible shackles of mind become tangible fetters of bondage.

I knew an unsuccessful physician steeped in self-pity. Daily she found her dearest wish, something to moan about. Disliking herself, she wanted to lose and engaged behaviors designed to ensure it. Another woman entertained submissive fantasies in the bedroom, finding oppression everywhere outside it. Another numerous and legendary type cursed me for every good I offered. On the conscious level they wanted the best for themselves, on a deeper, unconscious level only the worse, exorcising from their lives every person who promised otherwise. I examine just one category of perception—duality—ways the mind interprets sensory data, but all the categories raise questions of where the mind stops and the world begins, that is, the line distinguishing subjective reality from objective reality.

Simply put, subjective reality signifies something inside us and objective reality something outside us. Walking along the shores of the Aegean, one finds a vase rising from the sand, an objective reality. He or she then becomes stimulated beholding it, subjective reality. The flow of reality is inside-out. The object assumes objective reality after one perceives it subjectively; and further, every aspect he or she perceives resides in consciousness, never the object.

For example, when we perceive an object, a large boulder, say, we observe a heavy, tan object of erratic design but never the physical matter allegedly comprising it. Every aspect perceived resides in those observing and never that observed. A strongman hoists it easily while I struggle under its weight. I see tan and a colorblind person gray. Subjective reality is relative; every attribute inspires conflicting perceptions of those perceiving. If every characteristic we discern resides inside us, possibly the object has no reality outside us. We dream up a world by night; possibly we project one by day. The point is not the reality or unreality of the phenomenal world, but the questionable nature of objective reality and the mind's role in determining it. An erroneous notion circulates, holding reality pours into us from without; in truth, reality pours out of us from within.

Understanding this, I had to look within to uncover what undermined me without. The journey inward began with self-awareness. Having been run down since birth, reminded always of my shortcomings, real or imagined, I got into the habit of looking at myself, searching deeply for the monstrous defects assigned me. The ability to see and confront myself honestly, a high-degree of self-awareness, acted as a lens back on the world. The irony is the deeper we look in the further we see out. People who cannot see themselves harbor no understanding whatsoever, including the little taken to comprehend their own incomprehension. Self-unawareness keeps this mad doctor—and us—from exiting the merry-go-round. People resist seeing themselves because they don't want to confront the truth. I understood early the truth about humanity: We are a troubled race of mountainous baggage. Comprehension of this basic point helped me accept the worse about myself. Like Rasselas I met many suffering individuals shackled to confines of consciousness, experiencing misfortune of their own design, oblivious to the escape tunnel within their very cell. Without self-awareness one is sentenced to years of failure.

With it one's thinking sharpens, enabling him or her to see into others and life, and draw insights about both. All through my early years I endured harsh judgment and criticism. Biblical strictures as that against judgment represent not capricious injunctions but cautionary guidelines. Judgment of others invariably discloses condemnation of self. The people we judge symbolize us—a reflection of our own foul-ups, say. Consciously we see the foul-upies, unconsciously ourselves. Condemning them, we condemn ourselves, sowing our subconscious with censure and ultimately garnering that reality. I had a friend for whom I held nothing but contempt, coming over time to see he embodied everything I hated about myself. He acted as a self-imposed curse, just as I inadvertently jinxed those who condemned me, an unexpected reckoning that brought no small satisfaction in hindsight.

I have wondered if on death highly judgmental individuals remonstrate God for a grievous life only to be told they created it. Judgment demonstrates a form of preconceived notion, narrowing one's thinking and ultimately one's reality. Whenever I find myself condemning another, I ask a question: What does my verdict say about me? Judgment sentences us to the ruling of a presiding truth: The way we treat others determines how life treats us. Whether thoughts, whether actions, good or ill, we reap what we sow. The troubled doctor ridiculed a colleague's arrest only to find herself led away by the authorities. She mocked his troubled marriage; he worked it out and her own collapsed. I learned to be careful what I wished on myself. Always I found those steeped in judgment could be judged the harshest, much as those most in need of forgiveness never offer it. This brings me to another lesson learned:

If we fail to forgive others their trespasses, God denies forgiveness for ours. Christian, agnostic or atheist, an unforgiving heart inhibits the flow of blessings and power of prayer; for the necessity for forgiveness signifies an objective truth, a higher, prevailing truth outside human—subjective— experience. Greater truths govern our lives, bringing blessing or curse depending on our adherence to or

178

rejection of them. I count this realization among the most important of my life, and grasped it mostly through observing grief earned by abusive individuals around me. History remembers St. Anselm for the Ontological Argument, a logical proof for the existence of God. Objective truths furnish a better argument. We are accountable to a higher law and sentence or parole ourselves through that law.

I never became addicted to drugs, but engaged in many criminal acts to fund them, ripping off friends and family. A failed life inspires the worse, and for years I carried guilt for my actions, coming at last to a realization: All of us have injured someone. We release ourselves from wrongs done by us through forgiveness of wrongs done to us. A commuted sentence comes no other way. I found my unwillingness to forgive too often demonstrated an inability to forgive myself, inner thoughts again determining outer experience. At other times self-destructiveness inspired my withholding pardon: Any self-imposed sentence provided my enemies went down with me. Every time I served time in solitary. As with judgment all of us struggle with forgiveness. Danger comes from demanding its getting while denying its giving. I met many people who went easy on themselves, all the while holding others bitterly to their transgressions. Life imparts hard lessons for those imagining a double standard, an electric shock of sorts, intended to guide us from failure and to understanding.

My great escape from a ruined life, the knowledge gleaned along my getaway, skills required to traverse it and deceptions encountered to thwart it—my great escape demanded change, and specifically rebirth. Arts, humanities, life—all stress the importance of rebirth. Serious fiction and film always feature a rebirth scene, having three telltale images: A symbol of death, womb-like symbol of rebirth and character transformation. True love entails a dying to self and finding new life—rebirth—through another. The coffin and tomb signify classic symbols of rebirth, much as graceful statuary of so many classical goddesses, holding womb-like jugs. The symbol abounds, so what does it mean? It means this:

Something in one dies and he or she experiences rebirth into a different reality. One dies to drinking and is reborn a teetotaler, dies to excessive twinkies is reborn a slim person. Rebirth connotes the process of change, if not the process of life. Living life to the fullest involves not extravagant expenditure but an ongoing series of deaths and subsequent resurrections; and in fact resistance to change and resulting stagnation constitute a too common form of death, rendering virtual zombies under self-imposed curse. Life is death, and more specifically a series of deaths. I died to the old me to experience rebirth to a new me. Going back to self-awareness and the wider vision gained, I recognized the pervasive life pattern. Watching the Harry Potter films, I realized the Phoenix was a rebirth symbol, fire consuming the mythical avian that a new Phoenix rise from its passing. This myth as all myths communicates a truth: Life comes from death, good from evil, a new me from a wrecked me. I see the truth because I see myself. To overcome anything demands more than a hold on reality; it requires the ability to discern the truth. No one overcomes anything amidst unreality and lies. I died to live—again and again.

I died to self. Dying to self or ego means forsaking self-interests for the good of others. "In every period and in whatever society the supreme act is to give oneself, to lose oneself to find oneself.[i]" Losing oneself means slaying ego and self; finding oneself means awakening to the greater one, whether family, coworkers, a community, nation or world. I escaped hell by the same, considering always the needs of others. In doing so I furthered myself. I helped myself by denying myself. A lifetime in humanities convinces me dying to self constitutes a foundational principle in life. Christ died for us; we die to self, for others, that all of us live in him as one.

In times of weakness I lived for self, coming always to failure. Whatever the pursuit, one cannot achieve lasting success without weighing the good of others, a crucial point in my overcoming the past. Using people, hurting them, repaying evil for evil—deceptions and snares line the path out of imprisonment, with just one serving self and only self in a hard world. One cannot violate higher objective truths and win. Furthering self at expense of others always engenders disaster, another example of how life leads us from misunderstanding and to understanding.

The last point touches on an unexpected boon gotten from my journey. In college I studied literature and wrote critical papers on its interpretation. The novel conveys meaning more through symbol than with dialogue. A wardrobe, stargate or tunnel signifies the rebirth motif, for example, the passing from one reality to another, much as the newborn travels the birth canal, leaving a sheltered world for an altogether fallen one. Art imitates life with meaning wrapped in mundane circumstance and certainly tragic. Arthur never planned to free the sword from the stone; he stumbled upon it and tried it on a lark. Unseen forces led him there and lead us where we need to go. Lessons of kingship characterized his youth. Perhaps Dark Age punks usurped a teacher's authority, impressing on Arthur the necessity for strong, decisive rule. A reverence for justice arose from acts of injustice out on the playstone.

In my worse years I took up chess-playing, studied under three masters and advanced to a respectable level. Chess was an ark and shelter in a monstrous storm, giving me friends, acceptance and accomplishments in a time most needed. What's more, the game prepared me for later insight through deep plunges into mind the sport demands. Having long seen the rebirth motif in storytelling, I grasped its meaning running five miles a night to lose pounds and ask a girl out. Course scheduling in college pushed me out of the wrong major and into the English major intended for me. In an ironic reversal life prepared me for school as it rendered the ability to read between the lines, as it were.

Life clues, guides and instructs us; we only must interpret its symbols and follow its promptings. A scorned pariah, I began to perceive this mystical reality at a young age given vision that comes from suffering, if not solitary hours accompanying exile. I began to comprehend alternate reality was ultimate reality.

Looking for a spell or mantra out of a troubled life, I mined stories for insights, understanding they reflect on life and impart wisdom. Even spooky Gothic tales inform on life, the crypt signifying the subconscious, within which hollows fester all grotesque, horror and dread, rising at midnight to haunt the dream-world. The vampire casts no reflection in mirrors, having no reality outside consciousness. The obstacles impeding me resided within me. Crosses and sunlight drive off vampires. Christianity and the light of episteme—knowledge—repel dark inner impulses. I used both to hex mine. Many films see doomed characters helpless before evil. Hammer horrors present the actual truth: Evil cannot cross the threshold—of consciousness—without one's consent. I withdrew mine, having correctly interpreted the myth. Van Helsing represents reason and the count passion. My life vacillated between both, with reason and ensuing order gaining ground in time.

Allegorical of the struggle between good and evil, the film *Shane* presents good as frontier people who die to self for the greater one—the community— and evil as a man who lives for self at expense of the community. Living for self always entails a break with unity, and his death at film's conclusion demonstrates the ruin that comes from transgressing higher truths, a point stressed all through this essay. The truth will set you free and stories revealed many that helped me sidestep landmines, and one that led to my future.

In every tale, whether ancient myth or our modern mythos—literature and film—the hero follows a series of steps commonly known as the hero's journey. The Fellowship of the Ring enters the mines of Moria, much as Andy navigates a sewer birth canal in *The Shawshank Redemption*, both instances of one step in the heroic journey quest. The hero's journey reflects a life pattern. As the mythic hero I too undertook a harrowing, life-changing journey. I also denied the quest at times, at other times struggling with obstacles, monsters, bad guys and the arch villain—symbolic all of inner failings. As the hero I arrived at quests-end with a communal boon: To share with others my insights on life. Recognition of my purpose helped me overcome. Understanding of my heroism helped me overcome; for all who journey inwards, claymores at side, aided always by helpful spirit guides, whether tinmen, scarecrows or cowardly lions—all who journey in require courage to battle leviathans of consciousness. And all return with a communal boon. However agonizing my tale, I acquired knowledge and skills not gotten without a suffering passage through hell, and having them found my destiny.

I found eternal destiny. Some years back I began attending church following a fall. There I had an epiphany and undertook the one step required to become a saved Christian. As I pursued the Christian life a Spirit presence revealed itself to me, bringing further insight and revelation. Famine, exile and battlefield loss called the Hebrews into the covenant, just as God called me by suffering, turmoil and grief. They journey for the Promised Land in this world; I strive for the one in the next, the Bible a guidebook on how to get there without getting lost. With spiritual growth came blessings, a fallen financial state more prosperous, a suffering life more promising. For years I thought my life cursed but came to see it was blessed. God broke me as he broke the Hebrews because he loved me. Without a fall I would not have found redemption. Symbolic of the failed life, blind men and cripples carry the kingdom's message because healing, blessings and transformation of their lives testify to God's power. My life testifies to his power, going from a drugged mess and high school dropout to an honors university graduate and writer.

As the Book of Job, *Candide* and many other works, *Rasselas* addresses a foremost question in theology: The Problem of Evil, the dilemma of reconciling a good God with a suffering world. None of the many answers satisfactorily resolve the question, but my experience led me to these conclusions:

God called me by suffering. Thomas Aquinas gave just this answer to the vexing problem, with one negation having suffering less summons and more overkill. I counter by positing suffering kept my focus on the world to come. Philistines and Egyptians do not cross into the Promised Land; only God's chosen people—believers today—do, and I had to walk the path to get there. Suffering widened my vision. Suffering engendered within me compassion. Finally, suffering enabled me to clear my own head. The Pharisees expected a Messiah of political and military ambition. A teacher came instead, espousing ethics, divinity and fulfillment of prophecy. They missed the promised deliverance and bound themselves to a failed reality because they couldn't escape their own heads. The theme of *Forrest Gump* explores an eighteenth century answer to the Biblical Fall: Knowledge is corrupting. A dumb, innocent guy, by default submissive to God's will, finds every success, while smarter—fallen— characters flounder. God designed us to fulfill his perfect plan for our lives, but human thinking short-circuits that plan. My thinking had found no answers and exacerbated all problems. I looked outside my head for an answer, and found one for all eternity.

Silone, I. (1937). <u>Bread and Wine</u>. New York: Harper, p 289.

Mark A. Johnson

is a passionate inspirational speaker, certified Dream Coach and Dream Group Leader, and Toastmaster. He has given keynote and other presentations, impacting, encouraging, and empowering others lives in the process. Mark obtained his bachelors degree in Criminal Justice from Tennessee State University and Masters degree in Human Resources Development from Webster University.

Mark is a disabled veteran having served tours around the world. He has a community of self-mentality and actively works with the YMCA, Junior Achievement, and Boys and Girls Club of Lake and Sumter County. He is a Rotarian. He has also mentored in several local programs, the Micah Project of First Baptist Church of Leesburg, and the Childrens Home Society Model program. He is on the board of directors of The Daisy House Apopka, Florida for girls, Neighborhood Accountability Board, a community diversion program for at risk youth, and a facilitator of the Boys and Girls Club Passport to Manhood program for young teens. He is a past board of director of Habitat for Humanity of Greater Apopka.

Mark was awarded the Outstanding African American Citizen Award by the Fathers House Christian Center for 2008. He currently works for the Department of Justice, is the founder and CEO of Life To The Brim,

Multiple Streams of Success

and is Vice President of Johnson's Counseling Solutions. He is married to Antoinette together they have four children; Tanya, Prince, Robin, Kelly, and two grandchildren; Braylon and Brooklyn.

Contact information: mark@lifetothebrim.com.

Impacting the Space I Occupy

The purpose of life is to live a life of purpose.

Robert Byrne

My life's story truly embodies faith, hope, success, and multiple moments of overcoming adversity. I came from a middle class family and my parents were great providers. I considered myself blessed to experience the duality of a mother and a father with in my family. Mom was the fiber that held us together and always ensured we attended church every Sunday, which was instrumental in my spiritual growth. My father was a hard worker as well as my mom. I am the oldest of six children, four biological and two stepsiblings.

During my early teens, I belonged to a neighborhood group of guys affectionately called a gang. We managed to remain rather far under the radar, meaning we were no threat to anybody but ourselves. However, there was one event that took place early in my life I will never forget. God has spared my life multiple times in order for me to be used as an instrument of change. There is so much more to my story; however, the following chronicle of my life bears part of the witness to the miracle of my life's purpose.

Eddie and the Gun

The bullet always tell the truth
Man on Fire

The incident happened when I was 14 years old and worked for Mr. Poole, a local businessman who owned a hamburger shop and other interests in the neighborhood. He was a kind man who provided neighborhood kids the opportunity to earn money doing odd jobs. He was also the type of person who would lend money, find housing, or pay some poor person's utility bill. Mr. Poole was the ultimate manifestation of what I would call "unlimited random acts of kindness."

Nevertheless, one blustery spring day I was working in the Mr. Poole's corner hamburger shop by myself, until he returned from his errands. What happened next I will never forget for the rest of my life. As I was preparing the condiment tray, I heard the service bell ring and turned around to a .38 revolver pointed right smack dab in the center of my head. Not only was the barrel of the gun pointed at the center of my head but it was pressed into my skin. I saw each of the hollow point bullets in each chamber of the gun. I stood there asking myself, "Is this really happening."

I forget Eddie's last name, but he was a neighborhood bully that waited to jump guys when no one was around. He said, "Give me all your money." I said, "Eddie you can have this whole store if you want it, just take the gun outta my face." Time seemed to stand still, and then it started moving real slow. The entire moment was surreal.

I stood there in awe and absolute shock. This was happening to me! Many thoughts went through my head at that time, not to mention the thought of a bullet penetrating my skull and leaving my brain matter decorating the small corner restaurant interior. Other thoughts like "Am I going to die?" "Is he really going to do this?" "I'm still a kid. Man, this can't be happening!" "What will my family think?" "I will no longer be Daisy's boyfriend!" and the list went on.

I then saw myself in a casket, my family mourning my death, my friends walking past looking at me with sad looks in their eyes, tears streaming from their thoughts of "He was young like us." "That could have been me." I also wondered what the preacher was going to say and how he would say it. I thought about the little things I did in the dark that young mischievous kids do. Everything rushed through my mind. You have no idea. Only near-death experiences or some form of deep psychoanalyst can bring forth such thoughts and I experienced them all in the matter of minutes. How could so much go through one's mind at such a defining moment, I will never know, but it did. I even entertained the thought "He's joking!"

No soon after entertaining that thought than I watched his thumb cock the hammer of the pistol and I thought to myself, "He's going to shoot me." Then it happened! He pulled the trigger! And, there was a weird thump. For some reason I did not close my eyes. We stood there eyeballing each other for what seemed to be eternity. He then turned around and ran. I stood there for some time. I am not sure how long. I shook my head and continued working. My heart was racing and sweat profusely poured from my head. I believe I may have been experiencing some form of mild shock.

What sane person could stand there and keep working, not call the police, run for help or sound the alarm? I do not know. However, I do remember saying to myself, "I'm alive! I'm alive!" Strange as it may seem I never told my parents or Mr. Poole about the incident.

In fact, I continued to see Eddie in the neighborhood. He never said anything and neither did I. In fact, Eddie is dead now, like so many others I grew up with.

Since then I have had other significant life threatening events, both in the military and civilian life. I firmly believe that every harrowing experience we have and live through is a testimony to our life's purpose. It is God's way of saying, "Now listen here! I am not done with you yet! Here's another chance!"

I am excited that something phenomenal is happening within me. I decided sometime ago that I wanted my life to be of service; after all, I only have a short span of time left to make an impact. I have developed such a passion for life that I have never had before. Repeatedly, I have asked myself, "Why has it taken me so long to experience this feeling?" Yet, I already knew the answer. Everything in life is about timing. When I was younger, I would not have appreciated the lessons, pearls of wisdom, and various teachers who have crossed my path. Now that I am older and a bit more centered, I can now appreciate the wisdom King Solomon emphasized we obtain in the scriptures. Aha! Now I understand why it has taken me 51 years to figure it out. The true essence of life is about

Multiple Streams of Success

living on purpose. My ability to overcome adversity has been and continues to be centered upon a strong foundation of faith and in never losing hope of a better outcome, no matter what the situation. The aforementioned mindset has resulted in the various levels of success I have encountered along my journey of destiny and purpose.

When I operate in a spirit of being purposeful, I am not only edified, but those in the space I occupy are edified as well, which ripples and changes the world. I am a believer that once we have connected with our purpose; God will bring together everything we need in order to achieve it. Purpose often manifests itself in dreams. True dreams can never be shaken. They dominate your every thought. You visualize them prior to your eyes closing right before you drift off to sleep. You find yourself constantly sharing your dream (purpose) with those who will listen. The synergy of prayer, faith, hope, mediation, and action has helped me to overcome the adversities and vicissitudes of life and successfully obtain that which my spirit and passion yearn for.

I hardly ever listen to radio shows while driving, but while traveling to South Florida I happened across a conversation that caught my attention. Steve Harvey's radio show was on and he said something that really stuck in my mind. Mr. Harvey and his guest were talking about certain celebrities who fell down (experienced setbacks) and got back up (rebounded or were rebounding from their fall). He said something to the affect "that people instead of encouraging, tend to discourage, instead of uplifting they bring down." He referenced a comment that Patty Labelle's Aunt made regarding our gifts: "God gives us our gifts and does not take them away. We simply fail to use them." I strongly believe our gifts are also aligned to our purpose.

The Unfolding of My Purpose

Today when I think about my life's purpose, I know my first purpose is to worship my God. Afterwards, everything else will fall into place. It is at this point that I reflect on the abilities God gave me regarding helping people see the best in themselves. I cannot give someone what I do not have within myself. Therefore, if love does not abide in me, how can it resonate to others? It is the light within me that others see and are drawn towards. It is with this light that I positively impact the space I occupy. The last year and a half of my life has been unquestionably the most exciting. Once I began to focus on my purpose, God placed some of the most edifying people on my purpose driven path. Believe me certain people are seasonal. They come into our lives for a reason and when we recognize their purpose, we get it, or we do not. They could be in our life for five minutes, a week, a month, a year or longer. Either way, their path crossed ours in order to teach us a valuable lesson.

The receipt or benefit of that lesson is pursuant to our ability to be quiet, listen and be open to what is useful and releasing that which is not. Many of these people will stay within our circle and others will leave. Some of them may appear negative and others positive. We learn from all people. Our cups are either half-full or overflowing. I prefer to keep my cup half full in order to receive the wisdom life wishes to pour into my cup. Life is a process and we progressively experience each stage of the cycle in order to garner the sweet lessons it has for us.

During my twelve years in the military, I saw the best of humanity and the worst of humanity unfold before my eyes. I have found myself in the deserts of Egypt immediately following the assassination of Anwar Sadat, the Republic of the Philippines evacuating

Ferdinand and Imelda Marcos, and other places around the world I would never have dreamed of as a youth. I have participated in and supported numerous other operations I care not to discuss.

One day, while stationed at a remote air base in Turkey, I received a teletype inquiring if I was interested in an assignment at the United States Disciplinary Barracks (DB), Ft Leavenworth, Kansas. I thought about being back in the states with my son and family. I prayed about this decision and the question that surfaced in my mind was, "Where would I be the most benefit, in Turkey or in a prison working with incarcerated men and women?" Where would I be the most impact? The following scripture immediately came to mind:

> *"Remember them that are in bonds,*
> *as bound with them;*
> *and them which suffer adversity,*
> *as being yourselves also in the body.*
> *Hebrews 13:3 KJV*

The answer was plain and I accepted the assignment. Imagine going to the mall. I like the mall, because I like watching people. Different sizes, colors, mannerisms, occupations, single, married, etc. When you see these people, you have no idea what their real stories are, family problems, happy, sad, suicidal, terminally ill, etc. Even though I had dealt with people from diverse backgrounds and countries, I was not quite as prepared for this environment, this unique sea of humanity, as I thought. The United States Disciplinary Barracks was the military's only maximum-security facility in the world. Thirteen servicemen were on death row and others were serving sentences from two years to life.

Having never worked in a correctional setting I was certain I could remain fixated on the mission of security and the orderly running of the institution while positively impacting the inmates confined there. However, this was not the case initially. Developing an objective and non-judgmental attitude was not as simple as I thought. As I read the case files of the inmates assigned to my units, and absorbed the insights I received from Psychology, and other staff about these inmates, I began to feel this might not be the type of vocation I was cut out for. I could not believe some of the crimes these people had committed. The men and women locked up at the DB had committed all types of heinous crimes. They came from all around the world. I will never forget my first inductee into the system. The inmate was a soldier from Hawaii. He was a short stubby man with a large head, incarcerated for doing something to a child I prefer not share with you. Other inmates had placed an infant in a microwave, abused women in the most horrific manners, embezzled money, or killed their commanding officers. Whenever I looked at him and these other individuals, I hated them. Basic conversations with this soldier and other like him was out of the question, yet my mandate was to address the Hawaiian's, and the others incarcerated like him, concerns and ensure that he received whatever he had coming.

"Whatever they had coming" referred to anything according to policy to which they were entitled. Yet there were staff who could not separate their personal bias from their professional duty and would either go out of the way to not give them what they had coming or made life a little more miserable for them. I on the other hand was able to do it even though it was very difficult.

During the remainder of my time there, I did not impact the inmates as I thought I would, forgetting Hebrews 13:3, which was one of the primary reasons for my accepting the assignment. Yet, that was about to change!

The Federal Bureau of Prisons

I joined the Federal Bureau of Prisons (FBOP) in the early 1990's. My first assignment was at a facility in Tallahassee, FL. Up to this point; I had experienced my trial by fire at the DB and had learned much about the games inmates played. After being at the Tallahassee facility for about a year, an inmate walked along side of me one day and asked me, "Why do you work for a system that oppresses us?" I thought that a rather peculiar question, however, inmates in the military prison were different from those in the federal facilities.

All inmates watch staff like hawks. However, the mentality of those incarcerated in the FBOP was different. They had a higher propensity to determine who can be bought, who is scared, has family problems, is in need of physical and/or mental attention, who has it together, and who just does not. Actually, this process is germane to all correctional facilities.

The inmate that asked me the question was a Muslim. He was very articulate and had a very neat appearance in his prison garb. I enjoyed entertaining questions of that nature, and yet had no idea I was being nurtured by God to fulfill a higher purpose through my interactions with hardened men and women serving time behind the wall.

I told him, "Every man and woman is where they are because that is where they are supposed to be. Not every man or woman was born to be the President, CEO of a company, bank executive, college professor, trash collector, accountant, rapper, drug dealer, murderer, child molester, or nurse. We are where we are in order to learn a lesson", I then told him "You are most fortunate to have me here as an officer. I bring a normalcy to this place that many of you and others fail to appreciate. I allow you the opportunity to be treated with dignity and respect. Take for example this conversation, if you asked one of the other officers that question he may have been offended and wrote you up for insolence." I explained that prison is a society within a society and "I'm sure you would prefer to have someone working here that enjoys the work versus someone who hates everyday to step into this place."

He walked away and never approached me again. Many people on the outside feel inmates are unintelligent. However, this is far from the truth. My retort to a statement like that is, "Do not confuse intelligence with choices." I have supervised judges, accountants, lawyers, and doctors. Even Steve Madden, the shoe magnate occupied the same space I occupied within one of the institutions that I was assigned. He was one of individuals who positively impacted the space he occupied. There were a small number of incarcerated men who attempted to make a difference, and he was one. He was never egotistical and most polite.

Certain inmates, based upon their intellectual bent, taught classes, and he was one. There is nothing like helping those within the space you occupy. Tallahassee was a fertile learning ground for me.

Not only did I learn the characteristics and mindsets of inmates but I also developed relationships with many people that planted seeds of spiritual and mental edification into my being during my tenure there. One such person was David Duris, I count him today as one of my best male friends. Dave was one of many Case Managers at the Tallahassee facility. I was eventually promoted to Case Manager Trainee and assigned to Dave as a trainee. I could not help but notice the joy Dave exuded each day. We had similar spirits, but Dave was operating on a level I had not yet reached, but desired to obtain. He never entangled himself in gossip and the dynamics that so often adversely affects other staff members.

Dave treated everyone with respect and was likewise respected. I will never forget the day he told me "he didn't work for men, he worked for God, and when you work for God you give him your best. Therefore, it doesn't matter if your boss is looking at you or not, you do job to the best of your ability." His inner walk reflected on the outside and this is what resonated the loudest and commanded the respect of the inmates and staff alike.

I eventually began fellowshipping with Dave and continued to grow spiritually. A deeper change was taking place within me, one that I did not fight and, therefore, felt comfortable. I began reminiscing about my original reason for working in the correctional setting after separating from the military:

> *"Remember them that are in bonds,*
> *as bound with them;*
> *and them which suffer adversity,*
> *as being yourselves also in the body."*
> *Hebrews 13:3 KJV*

Part of my professional mission as a Case Manager was to help prepare inmates for release back into society. This was done primarily by challenging them to better themselves and not allow their mistakes to keep them in bondage. In simple language, "Use this as a learning experience and move on!" Therefore, I found myself encouraging them to participate in any class available and would mentor them as well as ensuring they did not do anything that would disrupt the orderly running of the institution.

I will never forget my first observations inmates graduating from the GED program. I was always happy to see men obtain their GED diploma prior to being released; however, on one particular day I shed tears when I saw a 65-year-old Black man walk up the aisle assisted by a cane to obtain his diploma. I do not why I was touched as much as I was; maybe it was because he reversed the old saying:

"You can't teach an old dog new tricks"
English 16th Century

Working from the Inside Out

During the remainder of my time at FCI Tallahassee, I considered myself an agent of change "Working From the Inside Out." I use the term Working From the Inside Out to mean changing the hearts and minds of men behind the bars. Once the change within has taken place, the transition back out is easier. A paradigm shift takes place and the chains that once held them back are broken. I tell people these inmates will be released one day and be your neighbor and mine.

Simply locking them up is not the answer. "Wouldn't you prefer they come out better than when they went in?" Everyone I present this question to agrees with my premise and appreciates my mission. I accomplished this mission by using positive communication skills and encouraging them to continue improving themselves by doing their time productively and not letting their time do them negatively. "Working from the Inside Out" is a reflection of my purpose. I do not judge them again, as they have already been sentenced by the judge, and therefore judged.

I allowed my actions to speak for me. They watched our mannerisms, the way we dressed, whether or not we took pride in ourselves, the way we communicated with their peers, and our own staff. It is what is not said that speaks loudly in the correctional setting. I interact with incarcerated men and women others would be afraid of or from whom they would turn their heads. I have spent a majority of my life behind bars, incarcerated with them, on a different level. It is a full-time job.

Multiple Streams of Success

I have spent most of my career helping them when they were sick, hurt, despondent; restrained them when they were a danger to others as well as themselves, and congratulated them when they achieved a milestone they never would have on the street. I am positively affecting them on the inside preparing many for the outside. This is what I was spared by God to do as a 14-year-old when that gun failed to discharge.

I eventually left the facility in Tallahassee and, after a brief stint in another state, ended up in a little town called Yazoo City, MS, the home of Zig Zigler and Jerry Clower. This is the second place God spoke poignantly to me regarding my purpose and destiny, adding a little more to my human toolbox of life. Yazoo City is between Jackson, MS, and Memphis, TN. The clay ground cracks in the summer, the heat is sweltering, and the mosquitoes are huge. The cat fishing was great, though!

Most of the locals are very warm in spirit. I lived in Yazoo City, not by choice, but necessity. I was a single parent at the time and needed to be close to my son. One day a retired postal worker from the church I attended, King Solomon Missionary Baptist Church, asked me if I was interested in going to the local jail to teach Sunday school. I thought this was a great idea, to help mentor incarcerated men and young adults. Many of them littered the street corners, having given up on their dreams. After a period it became more than Sunday school, but a moment of deep group facilitation. As time went on I saw young men and adults leave and come back into the jail. I wondered, "How could they come back to this place?" This facility, like many around the country, was in grave need of repair and was grossly overcrowded.

During one of our visits to the local jail, while talking with one of the inmates, my eyes began to tear up. I had a vision of such a strong magnitude that I was locked in a trance. The inmate tugged at my arm asking me if I was okay.

The vision had taken me to Rwanda where I began to visualize the butchering of the innocents, their bodies floating in the local river, and the displacement of thousands ravaged by war. Then I transitioned to Sarajevo and Kosovo, where the ethnic cleansing of other innocents had taken place. My trance briefly suspended me in Ireland where the Protestants and Catholics had dealt each other painful blows based on their differences. I shifted to the Middle East and then

Multiple Streams of Success

home, to America and the inner cities, suburbia and rural areas. Those within our society whose insensitivity to others ethic differences caused division, the poverty stricken and homeless, parentless children being raised by their grandparents and other caregivers, abandoned by mother and father either through incarceration or total abdication of responsibility.

The list of world and societal ills bombarded me within a moments time so hard that I felt no hope for humanity. After was shaken out of my trance by the inmate, I heard an inner voice resonate, "Mark, you cannot change the entire world, but you can impact the space you occupy, by changing the space you occupy, you change one person at a time. When you positively impact that person, they will impact someone else, and you have a rippling affect in action. Think about Christ, Gandhi, King, Teresa, Mandela, Gibran, da Vinci, and countless others that changed the world by impacting the space they occupied."

I never experienced anything like that before. Immediately the weight of sadness I experienced dissipated and was replaced with a new belief, "I cannot change the world, but I can positively impact the space I occupy." This space could be the within the institution or a local jail, at church, in a shopping center, standing in the grocery store line, talking to a youth or homeless person, or speaking to hundreds of people on stage.

I soon became very active in the local community, later visiting the local Job Corp organization with the aim of finding some alternative solutions to helping address the joblessness and truancy of the local youth problem. After touring the local Job Corp site and gaining a very deep understanding of their mission, I was able to facilitate getting young men signed up, trained, and employed through Job Corp. During my remaining time in Yazoo, I continued to espouse to the youth, "If you don't have a felony, dropped out of high school, don't know what you want to do, come with me and I'll get you in Job Corp!"

Back to Florida

One day my son said, "Dad I would love to go back to Florida and graduate." He was in the eleventh grade at that time. I prayed on the matter. I left it at the altar and was selected for the position for which I applied. "Positively impacting the space I occupied" became my new mantra in addition to "working from the inside out." Working from the inside out to me was part of my earthly purpose, realizing there would be others as

Multiple Streams of Success

I journeyed life's path. This assignment landed me at the largest federal facility in Florida, not only in Florida, but also in the United States. This was a vastly larger sea of incarcerated humanity than I had experienced before. I hit the ground running, again, working from the inside out. I realized the importance of keeping inmates productive not only encompassed employment (as they did work), but also programming.

My belief was that a productive inmate was, for the most part, a trouble free inmate and if they were trouble free then they contributed to the orderly running of the institution. Therefore, encouraging inmates to participate in institutional and unit-based programs was pivotal to them utilizing the necessary tools that assisted them in rehabilitating themselves, mentally, spiritually and physically.

There are many people in our society who feel incarcerating an individual automatically rehabilitates them. However, such common thinking is a common misconception within our society. There is an old saying:

> *"You can lead the horse to water*
> *but you cannot make it drink"*
> Unknown

As time went on, I began to take a deeper interest in the spiritual, mental, and physical development of certain inmates whose behavior and demeanor reflected "a cup half full." A cup half-full represents to me, a man or woman who is willing to learn something new and open to paradigm shifts. My platform was education and elevation of thought, the connection of the three circles: Mental, Spiritual and Physical.

I created and facilitated numerous programs, as the institution-favored inmates being productive and any program that legitimately contributed to their rehabilitation within policy guidelines. Now, there were times, when I just wanted to throw in the towel. Many inmates were incorrigible, appearing not capable of change, yet I would pray for them daily. Many would not appreciate any efforts to treat them humanely and respectfully. They would throw urine, feces, and other things at you. They repeatedly lied on you, acting as though you were the problem, when really you were the solution. There were an increasing number of inmates who would disrespect female staff by exposing their genitals. I communicated sternly with these men, vehemently explaining to them through parallels of how they would feel if someone did that to their mother,

214

sister, or even daughter. I have much respect for the women who work in this environment. They have to be as thick skinned as we men are, even thicker skinned. Many of the inmates understood my point and refrained, at least not openly in front of the female officers.

Each night I prayed for the inmates and their families. I repeatedly prayed for the staff that interacted with them and for myself. It really takes a special person to work in an environment of this nature. Moreover, I must admit, I love it. There is a stark difference between a job and career. Jobs pay the bills and careers change lives. There is a man named Paul in the scriptures who said, "Our lives should be a walking epistle," meaning our actions speak the loudest.

One moment touched my heart I must admit. It involved a 20-year-old black male whose name I cannot refer to due to privacy reasons. One day I spoke to the young man and he informed me he was in one of my units. I realized he had just been released from disciplinary segregation. I asked him why he was segregated, and before he answered I asked him, "Was it for code ***?" He then said, "What's wrong with it?" Code *** is the behavior I mentioned where inmates expose themselves to female staff.

This young man was serving a life sentence for committing a number of very heinous crimes. We had moment of intense communication following a programming session and he barged out. I had the officer bring him back in. I did apologize for appearing to jump to conclusions regarding the issue and told him, with tears swelling in my eyes, that I was not trying to be his daddy (Even though the common denominator for ninety percent of the inmates was an absent father.) I told him that I cared. As the tears began to swell in his eyes I told him the meeting was over.

I saw my son in him, another young African American male drifting in the sea of life, in a boat with no rudder. My son was older than he was, but this young man was serving a life sentence. There are many moments when the heart can do nothing but cry at the reality of incarceration. Many prisoners cannot believe another person could really care about their plight, yet I have to keep the hope that I can make a difference by impacting the space I occupy.

My continued journey of destiny and purpose continued moving upward when I joined the Foliage Toastmasters Club, in the neighboring city of Apopka, FL, in October 2006. It was between March 2007 and

March 2008 that I decided to strengthen my purpose of impacting people within the space I occupied. When I actively sought to better myself in order to be of better service to others, I met the following people who eclipsed my life and served as the glitter that has helped illuminate my purpose driven path: Marcia Wieder, America's Dream Coach; Les Brown, Motivational Speaker; Vernice Armour, America's first female African American Marine Combat Pilot; Kevin Bracy, dynamic speaker, author, and coach; and Amy Sellers, artist, author, and autism crusader, who really helped set the stage for what followed. Each one has impacted thousands of people within and outside of the space they occupy. I personally feel there is no way I would have met the preceding people, until I was ready to intensify the quest of my life's purpose.

> *"When the student is ready,*
> *the teacher will appear."*
> Title of Book by Black
> Comedian
> Calvin G Sims

The Inmates Dream Coach

I'll never forget the first time I received an e-mail from Marcia Wieder, CEO of Dream University. She was offering a special discount for friends of David Wood, an International Life Coach. I had purchased one of his workbooks some time ago, to gain a deeper understanding about this concept of life coaching. After reading her e-mail, I immediately knew this was the certification I needed to strengthen my speaking foundation. As a Toastmaster, I was learning to refine my speaking ability, but deep within my heart, I craved something more than just the ability to speak. I needed a process; something that I could use with my speaking that could impact those with which I communicate. After reading Marcia Wieder's objectives of Dream University and what being a Dream Coach entailed, I immediately enrolled.

I have taken my Life and Group Coaching to another level. I am now impacting the inmates at the penitentiary by taking them through the Dream Coach Group process. I enrolled Marcia in the idea and her support has made this possible. Many inmates did not know what Intention, Integrity, and Purpose were and how doubts and limiting beliefs could actually be an ally, if understood.

I chose some of the most difficult inmates in the institution and enrolled them in the group. Oh, I am not done yet! I will also provide an opportunity for this life coaching process to both the female and male inmates at the other facilities within the complex. They are beginning to understand that if they change their thoughts they can change their circumstances. That the ultimate dream is to live a life of purpose and that each man has a purpose that he was uniquely created to live.

Within the last year and one half I have learned a very valuable lesson regarding stories, that most people have one, some exciting, some not so exciting. Moreover, storytelling can be a very important aspect of connecting with people and helping them grow. Most people, inspirational and motivational speakers, professionals of all vocations, authors, evangelists, athletes, husbands, wives, children, grandparents, athletes, etc., have overcome some form of adversity in their lives. It is through our stories, filled with pain, joy, and triumph that we find our life's purpose and help others to find theirs. You may not be able to change the world, but you can positively impact the space you occupy.
